DON'T LET THE CANE FOOL YOU

How To Make A Comeback From Any Adversity

LOUIS MOORER III

authorHOUSE®

AuthorHouse™
1663 Liberty Drive
Bloomington, IN 47403
www.authorhouse.com
Phone: 833-262-8899

Published by AuthorHouse   02/27/2023

ISBN: 978-1-7283-7827-5 (sc)
ISBN: 978-1-7283-7825-1 (hc)
ISBN: 978-1-7283-7826-8 (e)

Library of Congress Control Number: 2023901219

Print information available on the last page.

Any people depicted in stock imagery provided by Getty Images are models, and such images are being used for illustrative purposes only.
Certain stock imagery © Getty Images.

This book is printed on acid-free paper.

Scripture quotations marked KJV are from the Holy Bible, King James Version (Authorized Version). First published in 1611. Quoted from the KJV Classic Reference Bible, Copyright © 1983 by The Zondervan Corporation.

Cover Design: Robbie Spencer Mathews (The Mathews Entrepreneur Group, Inc)
Coach: Michael Bart Mathews (The Mathews Entrepreneur Group, Inc)

CONTENTS

DON'T LET THE CANE FOOL YOU
HOW TO MAKE A COMEBACK FROM ANY ADVERSITY
THE COMEBACK EXPERT

For someone to describe himself as a *comeback expert* you would expect that there may have been some adversity and maybe some setbacks in life that would have caused difficulty and reasons to overcome some obstacles in order to accomplish greatness, or in many instances to remain in the land of the living. Of course, in his book, *The Comeback Expert*, Louis Moorer humbly and with genius describes his life and how he has comeback from impediments and tragedies that would have kept the best of us down for life. The greatness of this is when you share a conversation with him or work with him, you would never know what he has been through. However, that is not the end of the story, at least not for me. The expertise of this man is that he has the ability to look through your obstacles and setbacks and prepare you for your own comeback. He will draw you a roadmap, help you navigate it, stay with you until you reach your destination, and then come back to check on you to make sure that you are still on the right course. There are millions of people who can say they have overcome. There are few people who can sincerely and without judgment help you overcome. This book will do more than describe a life, it will *change* your life.

Dr. Lori-Renee Dixon James, *The Intentional Caregiver* **and** *President of The James M. Dixon Foundation, Inc.*

The bible says as a man thinketh, so is he…I have often heard the term "The Comeback," a very common statement of overcoming, returning, or beating the odds of something tragic. In his book, "The Comeback Expert: Don't Let the Cane Fool You," Louis Moorer, III shares experience(s) that makes him proudly wear or should I say own the title "The Comeback Expert." The reader gets a look at the whole man. It is effortless to revel in the good times, smile big when life is apple pie and ice cream, but when you are hit below the belt or sucker punched…learn what Louis does. Discover how you too can make a comeback.

-Yvetta "Doll" Franklin-Thomas
- Children's Author, Retired Educator

Make no mistake about it: The cane that supports Coach Louis' walk is symbolic of the support this man gives to those he counsels: he's strong enough to lean on; reliable enough to count on; and durable enough to talk and walk with you through any adversity you might be facing. So, DON'T LET THE CANE FOOL YOU!!! There's much more than meets the eye with Coach Louis. I'm a witness!!!!

Vickie Frazier-Williams MBA
Speaker, Financial Literacy Coach

ACKNOWLEDGMENTS

This book is the result of tremendous love, commitment, and support. I would like first to acknowledge my Lord and Savior, Jesus Christ, because, with Him, ALL things are possible! I want to acknowledge and thank my beautiful wife, Shanay, who has stood by my side every step of the way. She is my biggest supporter and cheerleader who tirelessly assists, challenges, and often speaks life into me. I would also like to acknowledge my mentor of 12 years, Andy Henriquez, who continues to motivate and inspire not just myself, but so many others who have had the pleasure to be in his presence. To Star Bobatoon, thank you for being an excellent example of a good coach and trainer. I would be remiss if I didn't acknowledge Tiger Sun for his creative genius, while Andy has also become an important piece of The Comeback Expert Brand.

To my prayer partner Sister Marion Y. Winters and dear friend Sister Yvetta Doll Franklin-Thomas, I thank you for constantly reminding me that Christ is the source and that there's nothing we cannot do with Him in our lives. Your unconditional support and encouragement are greatly appreciated.

Last but certainly not least, I'd like to thank the Show Up For Your Life Movement members and The Master Storyteller Academy & Mastermind for your ongoing support and encouragement. More importantly, for reminding me every day of the significance of my work. To all of you, I sincerely thank you!

FOREWORD

Throughout our lives, we will all experience hardships and difficulties. However, what sets us apart is how we react to these challenges. We can let our outer circumstances control us, or we can have power over them and gain a better understanding of ourselves.

I remember when I left my corporate job as an accountant to pursue my dream of becoming an entrepreneur and professional speaker in December 2004. I was convinced the transition would be smooth, but I quickly realized I had underestimated the process. To make matters worse, I invested all my savings into a real estate project in Costa Rica that failed terribly. I was devastated. I now had no job, no savings, and I practically had no hope. This was my first significant setback as an entrepreneur, and I was desperate for a comeback. It took me years to mentally and financially recover after I almost gave up on my dream.

Like many people, I faced several challenges and setbacks throughout my life. If only I had someone who could guide me through those tough times! That's why Louis Moorer III wrote this book - to inspire and guide anyone facing a challenge or setback. This book is full of helpful advice to assist you in making a comeback in your life.

Louis has had the ultimate setback, which should have shattered his will and crushed his spirit, but he has rallied to orchestrate a stunning comeback that has spanned two decades. Louis not only discusses his challenges and ordeals in this book but also offers a roadmap for regaining your former glory no matter what life throws at you.

You will feel motivated and guided by Louis as he helps you change your perspective and become victorious no matter what life has thrown at you. The inspirational stories shared in this book will take you from feeling helpless to feeling capable of bouncing back from your most difficult circumstances.

This book is the first step toward reclaiming your life. You are unstoppable from now on because what you need to win is within these pages. In Louis' words, "When life knocks you down, you don't have to stay there." It's time to fight back.

-**Andy Henriquez**
Speaker, Business Storytelling Coach
Author of Show Up For Your Life

INTRODUCTION

Life is a process of trial and error. As we go through life, we will be dealt with many life-altering occurrences that set us back. However, I believe we can make a comeback with anything we face. It can often be a relationship, finances, health, or your goals and dreams.

When a setback occurs, we have to decide to make a comeback in our lives. Making a comeback is merely (you) deciding to motor through the situation in the event you will overcome and get back to the best version of yourself. As you read on, keep this pro tip in mind, It's Time To Get Serious – And Find Your Moment of Clarity. Making a comeback will require you to harness the power of purpose. Give serious thought to what your purpose in life is. Knowing your purpose is one of several keys to making a comeback in your life.

I started making a comeback at the early age of 9 months due to being diagnosed with having a hole in my heart. I had to undergo surgery at a very early age. Doing so gave me the will to fight, and it's been in me ever since. I've had to make numerous comebacks in my life. The world teaches you to moan, groan, and complain when you have a setback. However, I know that you must decide if you want to make a comeback. I know you will receive my blueprint for making your comeback because you are reading this book.

When I faced adversity, I overcame it with courage, perseverance, and tenacity. I was able to do that over and over again because of my ongoing personal investment in myself. I invested in hard & soft cover books, audiobooks, seminars, and coaching. They are all significant components of developing a positive mental attitude and mindset. Creating your personal-development habits can enable you to do what others are unwilling to do to get the results others won't have.

If you are looking to make a comeback in your life and take your life to the next level, I highly encourage you to invest in yourself by reading this book more than once. Life is filled with challenges and uncertainty. Building the foundation of knowing what's required of you will only make it easier for you as you set out on a quest to make a comeback in your life.

Let's start by pressing the reset button, and start today with making that needed comeback in your life. Let the journey begin!

CHAPTER 1

"WHEN LIFE KNOCKS YOU DOWN, YOU DON'T HAVE TO STAY THERE"

~Louis Moorer III~

I want to talk to you about the adversity of taking hits. My use of the word 'HIT' can mean various things, for example, an impact or collision, setbacks, trials, tribulations, losses, and facing any unexpected 'HIT' that happens to you unexpectantly. One thing I know for sure is that as you go through life, you will experience some hits. You will encounter some 'HITS' when it comes to your health. You will encounter some 'HITS' when it comes to your relationships. You will encounter some 'HITS' when it comes to your finances. You will encounter some 'HITS' when it comes to your goals and dreams. The question is, how will you deal with the HITS? One of my favorite quotes is by Rocky Balboa, who says, "Life is not about how hard you hit; it's about how hard you get hit and keep pushing forward. It's about how much you can take and keep pushing forward!" Through every adversity, there is a seed of greatness.

I remember when I was in elementary school, I took on a lot of different character traits (not necessarily positive ones), meaning I was a class clown. Yet, at the same time, I was also quick-tempered and what most of my teachers considered me to be: A problem child! I was more concerned with making my classmates laugh than doing schoolwork. When we would go outside to play, I would fight the other kids instead of having a productive recess. Every teacher would see me coming into their class, and they would say, "Oh my gosh, NOT Louis again!" I was disciplined by my teacher on more than one occasion. One time, the teacher disciplined me in front of my entire class. Embarrassed, I knocked over my teacher's desk. Eventually, my teacher sent me to the principal's office because I was disruptive in class. The principal said, "Louis, we have attempted to work with you several times, and you continuously demonstrate a lack of discipline. I'm sorry to tell you, Louis, you are expelled from this school." I was in disbelief. I didn't know what to say.

My parents came to my school to meet with the principal. That was an embarrassing moment for me because I knew they were paying tuition for me to have the best education, and I felt at that moment that I had let them down.

After laying in my bed later that night crying from the shock that not only had I been expelled from my school, but I would also be placed in a remedial class. I heard the words 'I would be in remedial classes,' but I chose not to accept those words. I spent several years proving to teachers that being in a remedial class was unnecessary and that I didn't belong there. Finally, I was on top of my schoolwork, made good grades, and listened to the teachers when given instructions.

It was necessary (for me) to share my early childhood

experience of how I dealt with a life situation and decided not to stay there. Now that I am an adult, that experience played an integral part in helping me face the biggest challenge in my life.

I will never forget this day back on July 5th, 2003. It was a beautiful warm sunny day to ride my motorcycle. The sky was clear, with no rain in sight. The trees were whistling in the wind as the youthful sounds of little children were playing everywhere. I left my house, and I was on my way to see my older cousin Steve because I admired him as a teenager. Steve always had the things I wanted in life, especially a motorcycle. Steve had a motorcycle, and I wanted to show him my prize motorcycle on that faithful day. This was no ordinary motorcycle; it was a purple and white Honda CBR 600cc. It was marketed as one of Honda's top-of-the-line, middleweight racing bikes. As I was cruising down Paseo Padre Street in Hayward, CA, enjoying the warm rays of the sun beaming down upon me, with the wind blowing in my face. I observed a car was about to swerve out of control and into my lane! I immediately recalled an earlier incident back in 2000 when a lady ran a stop sign and hit me. That was an unwanted flashback that was presently reoccurring. It was like I was traveling back in time, reliving that HIT.

As I continued riding my motorcycle, I overreacted and veered too close to the curb. I HIT the curb, fell off my motorcycle, and landed in a flower bed. I looked up at the clear blue sky, saying to myself, "Louis! Get up! Get up, man!" I DID get up. I thought I was okay. However, after taking one step, I fell, landing back in the flowerbed. Once again, I was looking up at the clear blue sky.

Within minutes a small crowd gathered nearby, and there were several people that witnessed the accident were present. In my time of need, these Good Samaritans came to my assistance. I remember someone in the crowd asking me, "Do you have someone you can call?" I said, "Yes," and I pointed to my cell phone that was nearby. "Call my older sister, Tracy!" A Good Samaritan took the liberty to call my sister, and shortly after, the ambulance came. One of the paramedics placed a mask over my mouth. These Good Samaritans were God-sent Angels to watch over me because I had just taken another HIT in life. That was the last thing I remembered. I don't remember hearing the blaring sounds of the ambulance. I don't remember the paramedics giving me medical care or strapping me on a gurney or stretcher, loading me into the ambulance, and whisking me away to the emergency room.

I woke up in a hospital bed with my family beside me in the room. There was uncertainty in the air, and I had no idea what was happening. "Beep! Beep! Beep!" I can hear the sounds in the background coming from the monitors that were connected to me. As my Mother watched me open my eyes, she grabbed my hand and stroked my forehead, and to my surprise, she said, "Baby, you've been in a serious motorcycle accident. You're going to need surgery!" Then, my younger sister La Wanda said, "Louis, can you move your toes?" I tried, but I couldn't move them. The family looks at one another in shock and disbelief. My Mother is at my bedside, holding my hand. I wanted to reach up and hug her, but I couldn't move. Finally, my Mother said, "Baby, lay here. You're going to have surgery."

Naturally, I went into surgery, which took about 8 hours. Rods and screws were surgically implanted in my back for stability. Thankfully, the surgery was very successful. I found myself in my hospital room praying, thanking God that I was still here, thanking God He didn't take my life after the dreadful HIT.

Then, I heard a voice say to me, "This is your doctor from the surgery. Do you mind if I talk to you?" I responded, "Yes, you can talk to me Doc." The doctor says, "Louis, great news! Your surgery was successful, but I must be honest: you broke your ribs and punctured your spinal cord." The doctor then says something that I will never-ever forget. He said, "Louis, you may never walk again." I lay in bed with tears falling from my eyes. I started to ask myself a host of questions: Will I ever play basketball again? Will I ever dance again?

After listening to the doctor telling me that I'd never walk again, the doctor also said that I would never be able to work. Finally, he told me that I would be eligible to receive disability. The amount would have been $1600 per month. Let me ask YOU a question: would you settle for $1600 per month if you knew you had more inside you that was capable of more than a $1600 lifestyle that would only erode your life, liberty, and the pursuit of happiness and success?

I reflected on a quote by Les Brown – "You may be given a word, but it's up to you to accept the word." Here's what I know: Many people have been given the word that there is no money to be made in this economy. You go to the doctor for a routine checkup and are diagnosed with a severe health issue. The love of your life walks into the room and says, "I no longer want to be in this relationship." Although you were given the word, it's up to you to accept it. Through every adversity, there is a seed of greatness! I was determined to find my seed of greatness.

I was in the hospital for over a month and a half recovering from a traumatic hit. While having a conversation with myself, I was also visualizing where I could be if I became fully committed to my rehabilitation. I reflected on many people who have been in challenging situations and what they did to make a comeback in their life. So, I took my recovery efforts one day at a time. I needed to do whatever my rehab specialist asked me to do. Over time, I saw myself improve, and the belief started to kick in. Earl Nightingale – "We become what we believe." I believed 20 years ago and still believe today that I will walk without a cane!

So, as you continue to read this book, there will be times in your life when you have to make critical decisions about how you want to move forward during and after you take a HIT. I know from experience that the best way is seeing yourself rehabilitated and aligning yourself with the right people who can assist you in getting there.

To this day, it's been 20 years since I didn't accept the words "never walk again." I went from a wheelchair to a walker. From a walker to a quad cane, and as I continued my recovery, today, as I write this book, I am walking with a single cane. I'm not going to stop until I'm walking without assistance! Throughout my life, I learned nothing is impossible for a man or woman who will not quit on their goals, dreams, and other important things. So let's break up the word Impossible to I'm Possible—one word with two different meanings. I like I'm Possible.

Rocky Balboa says, "Life is not about how hard you HIT; it's about how hard you get HIT and keep pushing forward. It's about how much you can take and keep pushing forward!" Don't we know that all too well? This quote has been my anchor in making a comeback in my life. I'm excited for you because if you're reading this book, there's a comeback in your life that you are or should be determined to make!

Although being in a motorcycle accident has been a massive challenge in my life, I believe that the experiences I endured prepared me to stay committed to my recovery to walk without assistance.

It's not what happens to you in life; it's how you respond to it that counts. There are many more experiences that I could share with you; however, I believe that you get my point that I'm trying to drive home. In life, situations will happen to you, and you may feel like you've been knocked down during and after taking the HIT. However, you have a choice to make. The choice I want to leave you with is this: WHEN LIFE KNOCKS YOU DOWN, YOU DON'T HAVE TO STAY THERE!

CHAPTER 2

"WHEN YOU GET KNOCKED DOWN, ASSESS YOUR SITUATION QUICKLY & HONESTLY"

~Louis Moorer III~

Seven months after returning home from the hospital, I was standing up in the bathroom doorway, holding on to the walls doing whatever I could to produce strength in my legs. Finally, my legs began to fatigue and gave out. BOOM! I HIT the floor. Immediately, I crawled over to the bed and pulled myself up to sit on the bed. I was in disbelief that my legs gave out on me, but reality set in. I wasn't strong enough to stand on my own two feet. Unfortunately, sometimes in our life, we get knocked down, and we don't take the time to assess our situation honestly so we can get back on our feet.

Although I stood in the doorway and my legs gave out, I knew I had to continue doing something because life waits for no one and neither does opportunity. My mother prepared a meal for me and asked me to come into the family room to eat it. As I began to eat, an ad came across the tv screen. ATMs for sale. I got excited, wrote down the number, and told myself, 'when I finish eating, I'm going to make this phone call!' Following my meal, I called the number, and someone picked up. I inquired about the ATM ads that I had just seen. They scheduled a call with one of the top representatives to speak with me. The next day, the top representative called me and shared the opportunity to make money in department and grocery stores using these ATMs.

I was elated! I was thinking of ways to invest in holistic medicines as it was becoming expensive to maintain on my own. However, the investment in the ATMs was more than I anticipated. Who could I call to partner with in this endeavor? I called my brother, Travis. I shared with him that we have made many prior investments together. Finally, I shared with Travis the opportunity I had found. He was willing to consider a partnership if I could arrange a 3-way call with the representative. We made the call and started our ATM investment due diligence conversation.

The representative assured us that, financially speaking, this was an excellent opportunity and that we could make a lucrative income from it. So we decided to start with a $15,000 investment in 5 ATMs. The machines were placed in Northern California. The 1st month, we made $500, and I was starting to say," Yes!" This will definitely assist me with getting the herbs and essentials I need for my recovery!" In the second month, we made $300. At this point, I told myself we didn't make $500, but we still made a profit. However, by the 3rd month, we only made $40! I'm telling myself, "This is not the lucrative income we were told we could make."

The 4th month came around, and we didn't make ANYTHING!

However, I knew I could call the customer service number if we had any questions. I quickly dialed the number only to receive the familiar phrase that we have all heard at one point in time on the other end: The number that you have dialed has been disconnected. I'm saying to myself, "This is not the lucrative income they proclaimed we could make!" I also remember being provided with an additional customer service number in case of an emergency. I immediately called the second number. When I did, a woman answered and said, "This business is no longer in business. It's a scam!" I could not believe what I had just heard!

I immediately felt defeated, but then I reflected on a quote by Maya Angelou – "In life, you will encounter defeats, but you must not be defeated." So, although being knocked down, I stopped to assess my situation. I told myself, "This did not work out the way I wanted, but what can I learn from this situation?" It's important to be a person who does his due diligence and understands business is about taking risks. No risk, no reward. I cannot be successful being afraid to take risks or not seek counsel from people who have achieved success in their personal and business lives.

From that point forward, I began to immerse myself in personal development. I developed a burning desire to grow at the core. As many of you are reading this section and acknowledged that you got knocked down, you might need to assess your situation before moving forward.

A good friend of mine was going through a divorce. This was hard on him, and he was dealing with all the emotions that came with that experience. I turned to him and said, "I know you feel knocked down, but I want you to assess your situation." I asked him, "What could you have done differently or better as a husband?" He responded, "I could have communicated better and not suppressed my feelings when I knew this was not the pattern of success for our marriage." I commended him for being transparent with himself and with me.

When we go through life and deal with adversities, especially when we get knocked down, it's essential to stop and realistically assess our situation. Being The Comeback Expert, I stopped to evaluate my situation many times, and because of thinking things through and not reacting from emotion, great things have happened in my life. One of the greatest things that happened in my life when I got knocked down after evaluating my situation is I found courage. Finding the courage to evaluate your situation when you know things are not working out for you is the greatest gift you can give yourself.

When I faced adversity, I had to be honest with myself. I knew I had to do something about it. My courage played a big part in the outcome. There's nothing more refreshing than when you're up against adversity, and you have the courage to do something about it and put yourself in a better position. I always tell my clients to put themselves in a position of power and not a position of dependency.

On a more personal note, my wife and I were trying to conceive our baby several years ago. Unfortunately, we were unsuccessful after a couple of years despite seeking medical assistance. After assessing our situation, my wife looked into improving our diet to increase our chances of conception. We pivoted and adopted a vegan nutritional lifestyle as a new approach, and within three months of a vegan lifestyle, my wife found out that she was pregnant! Learning that we were about to become parents was an indescribable feeling. We were elated.

Having a child is a rewarding experience and a serious responsibility at the same time. Speaking about my wife, after she gave birth to our beautiful daughter and received clearance from her doctor that it was safe to resume her diet and exercise, she began her journey in an attempt to lose her postpartum weight. After several attempts at her usual approach to weight loss, her efforts were ineffective. As a result, she assessed her situation and sought out other options. After extensive research, she learned about the benefits of Intermittent Fasting and began implementing this practice into her weight loss journey. After she set a goal of losing 45 pounds, she surpassed her goal in roughly six months. More importantly, she has maintained her goal three years later.

My wife shared with me in detail about Intermittent Fasting, and it made sense after observing her not eating at certain times. When I asked my wife were there other benefits to Intermittent Fasting other than weight loss, she emphatically expressed, yes! A short while after, I was inspired to implement Intermittent Fasting into my own regimen. Now, I too share the information with others who are open-minded and want optimal health in their life. My wife and I were willing to make a difference in our health because we assessed our situation when we got knocked down. If we can do it, you can too!

The many trials of life will knock you down so many times, and when it does, that is the time not to react but to respond and ask yourself the question: What do I have to do to get myself out of this situation? Life is full of occurrences that will test you. When life tests you, you can rise to the occasion or allow the challenge to stagnate you. Pam Morris says, "If something is strong enough to bring you down, show them you're strong enough to get up!"

In 2010, I was having dinner with my girlfriend at the time. All of a sudden, my cellphone vibrates. At first, I wasn't going to answer because we were really-enjoying ourselves. Then, something told me to answer my phone. When I answered, I got a frantic voice on the other line saying, "Louis, this is Joanne, your neighbor! Your house is on fire!" I responded, "What? My house is on fire?!" I looked at my girlfriend and told her I had just received a call that my house was on fire. Immediately, I left our money for our dinner on the table, and we ran out of the restaurant. I sped home as fast as possible, and I knew my girlfriend was a little scared from how fast I was driving. Thankfully, I didn't have an accident or get a speeding ticket! After pulling up to my home, I witnessed all of my neighbors outside. I said to myself, "This does NOT look good!" I attempted to open my garage door from my car, but it would not open.

I got out of the car, and I was able to open the front door, and when I did...POOF! Smoke came rushing out. I went upstairs and saw the indoor sprinkler system spraying water continuously. Minutes later, the fire department showed up and shut the water off. When the fire department went upstairs, they discovered that I had left a candle burning which was the cause of the fire. They told me that the chemicals present due to the fire were too hazardous to inhale and that it would be unsafe to stay there. I was advised to stay at a hotel until the fire damage was resolved.

My girlfriend and I checked into a hotel, and I was stressed out due to the situation. However, I thought to myself: What's the good in this situation? I acknowledged that I had homeowner's insurance, no one got hurt, and I thought I had a supportive girlfriend. With that, I managed to get some sleep.

I was awakened early the next day by my girlfriend, and she said, "Can we talk?" I said, "Yes, what would you like to talk about?" She said, "Louis, I can't be in this relationship anymore." I said, "Excuse me?" She said again, "Louis, I can't be in this relationship anymore." After saying that, she just left the room. This is a perfect example of something trying to bring me down because of the fire. I had to show that I was strong enough to get back up. In doing so, my home was not only restored, but I am now a devoted husband and father to my loving wife and beautiful daughter!

My first challenge to you is to acknowledge when you have been knocked down and always be willing to assess your situation. My second challenge is that you must be willing to have the courage to do something about your adversity so that you can always make a comeback in your life.

CHAPTER 3

"KEEP MOVING FORWARD"

~Louis Moorer III ~

Dr. Martin Luther King Jr. – "If you can't fly, then run. If you can't run, then walk. If you can't walk, then crawl. But whatever you do, keep moving forward." My cousin Kevin, is also my Alpha Phi Alpha fraternity brother, reminded me of this because he acknowledged I was not being my best self. I was at a point in my life where I began putting my life on hold. Instead of going out as I usually did, I would stay at home because I was still dealing with the aftermath of my motorcycle accident. Kevin always told me, "Life waits for no one, and neither does opportunity." He would say these words because he knew that I was not living up to my full potential.

He was absolutely right because, in our early twenties, we bought real estate and changed the lives of so many people, including my own. I was in a position where I was able to purchase my first luxury vehicle. I would drive it all the time. However, after my accident, I chose not to drive and told myself, "Once I'm walking again, I'll drive it. Kevin called me out about the fact that I was getting away from myself. He reminded me to keep pushing forward despite the setbacks and disappointments. Keep moving forward means being willing to continue even during great times of difficulty.

I know that if you keep moving forward, the obstacles in your life, whether big or small, you can overcome them. Developing your strong desire not to let external circumstances stop you from pursuing your goals and dreams should become your new mission. I took what Kevin told me to heart and realized that I was letting life pass me by. I was so immersed in my recovery that I allowed that to take over. One day, I finally took action and got behind the wheel after 18 months of 'waiting.' Getting behind the wheel gave me hope and inspiration to keep pushing forward because I was walking when I first purchased the vehicle. It might not be a car for you, but perhaps a life circumstance, a financial situation, or even a relationship. Whatever you do, you have to keep moving forward!

I have taught, trained, and inspired people to keep moving forward because when you move forward, it gives you a new perspective. A new perspective gives you a new outlook on life.

One of my clients called me and said, "Louis, my wife left me for another man." I got quiet. He continued to say how he couldn't believe she had left him after how long they had been married. I responded with, "I know you're hurting. I know you feel life is over because of your long history with your wife." I replied, "I know that, unfortunately, the marriage is over, but you must keep moving forward." He agreed, and he let out his last cry. I didn't hear from him for a couple of months. When we eventually talked, he thanked me for the honest conversation and advice. He has pushed through his grief and has started a new life for himself.

I know it's not easy to start over, and sometimes people do not have the desire to keep moving forward after a divorce. However, in order to make a comeback, you have to see yourself moving on from that situation and visualizing where you can be. Know that it can happen to you. Yes, it can! Your energy and focus have to be placed on the new outcome that you want for yourself. Once you can visualize your results, the joy from starting over and knowing you're about to make a comeback will inspire and motivate your journey as you look forward to better days ahead! I use this concept while coaching many others and helping my clients process their journey moving forward. The one thing I wanted them to know is that starting over isn't a bad thing. It's good for the soul and spirit.

When you choose to move forward, you can discover a renewed sense of hope for your future because you feel excited about the comeback you're about to make in your life. However, having hope can be challenging if you allow yourself to park. Dr. Maya Angelou says, "People go so far, and then they park." Unfortunately, people park because of fear and a lack of faith.

In 1965, my parents purchased their 1st home where I grew up. My parents bought it for $14,000! At that time, one might consider that to be a lot of money, but today that same house that my parents bought for $14,000 is worth over a million dollars. I was intrigued by the increase in property value, and I asked my Dad why he didn't purchase any additional homes. He responded, "I didn't know the property value would increase this much." Knowing my Father, this was his way of saying he didn't fully understand real estate. So instead, he chose to park, just like the quote by Maya Angelou mentioned earlier.

In today's time, I believe because of one's personal development and mindset, people might start one way, and they can be completely different in five years if they choose to use discipline to get ahead. However, if one does not use discipline and their desire to move forward is not strong enough, one will always be stuck in park. Therefore, as you continue through life and you find yourself being afraid and unsure of your future, you must be willing to keep moving forward. Do not settle for your life staying in the park position! Think about your life not moving forward like a parked vehicle in a driveway. When a car is in the park position, it will not move, even though the driveway has a clear path. When your life is in the park position, you will not move forward unless you map out a clear path for achievement and make the paradigm shift to the drive or moving forward position!

I have a question for you to contemplate: As you read this book, what are some things you know that you need to keep moving forward on? STOP! Take about five minutes and begin writing your list now. Use the man in the mirror approach and be brutally honest with the reflection that's staring back at you. Remember, you can fool some people sometimes; however, if you are good enough to fool yourself by not accepting that you must change certain things in your life if you expect to get out of the park position and move forward in life, you are not being rational!

Now that you're back, the one or many things you acknowledge you need to move forward will only assist you with getting ahead. Instead of hiding behind barriers that are preventing you from being that amazing person God has designed you to be, have faith and courage to do what it takes to move forward.

In making several comebacks in my life, I'm so proud that I kept moving forward when I was up against the opposition of being in remedial classes, knowing I shouldn't be here. It could have been an excuse for me to park in that remedial class and not fight to move forward. As I spend time with you, I know this is one of the biggest areas in our lives where we don't see the importance of moving forward when dealing with real-life situations. Instead, 90% of the population will park, moan, groan, and have a defeated mindset. That doesn't have to be you!

For the sake of keep moving forward, when I previously shared with you that my girlfriend at the time left me at a critical time when my house caught on fire, that was a defining moment for me. I'm so thankful that I kept moving forward, and because of that, I'm now happily married to the love of my life and have a beautiful daughter. Throughout my years of making several comebacks, I learned that my faith has always gotten me through. I cannot let what I SEE make me forget what God SAID He would do.

I want you to get in the driver's seat when making a comeback in your life. No longer will you park when up against opposition, challenges, and setbacks. Instead, you will travel the path to becoming the best version of yourself that you can be. The one thing I will guarantee, if you always choose to keep moving forward, you will discover some things about yourself that will make you say, "Wow! I didn't know this was possible for me!"

Finding out what's possible for you, your new reality is you're always going to want to break the spirit of being average and commit to becoming better. Your willingness to keep moving forward will set you apart from ordinary to extraordinary. The true winners in life are the ones who don't allow unforeseen circumstances to derail them from accomplishing what truly matters to them. I commend you for the desire for wanting to adopt a new mindset to move forward in your life.

CHAPTER 4

"HAVING THE CONFIDENCE TO MAKE A COMEBACK"

~Louis Moorer III~

Nothing is noble about feeling defeated!!! However, having the confidence to make a comeback is essential to the process. When I graduated from high school, the guidance counselor told my mother that I was not college material and that I should pick a trade for my career. My mother told me about his suggestion. I strongly disagreed because I knew I had the confidence to pursue-higher education and live a productive life. With that, I pursued college at a four-year state university.

As I stated earlier, I was distracted and fell off, but that was a wake-up call. Immediately, I began to make a comeback in my life because I had faith that I had what it took to succeed. As I continued through college, I received A's and B's. Receiving good grades strengthened my desire and outlook about my ability to accomplish anything I set my mind to achieve, despite the naysayers. From this experience, it became apparent to me that to recover from any situation, the one thing necessary is having self-confidence and taking intentional action.

We're living in a time where so many people aren't living from a place of surety. Instead, they are living in a place of uncertainty. That's why today, so many doubt themselves. Les Brown says, "In choosing your future, the first principle is it's possible." A principle starts with developing confidence because you believe you can, instead of thinking it can't happen. Unfortunately, I've witnessed many people talk themselves out of opportunities and not pursue their goals and dreams because they didn't believe it was possible. As a result, they were not willing to make a comeback in their lives.

When I first met my wife, we met online. She was getting to know someone else while also getting to know me. She was transparent in telling me so. I was also transparent in sharing my recovery process from my motorcycle accident with her. She said that she appreciated my honesty. As time progressed, I knew I could see myself with this woman for the rest of my life. I expressed my desire for us to become more exclusive. At that point, she obliged. However, she shared some reservations she had due to her getting hurt in the past. Eventually, as we continued to spend more time together, she expressed that she felt that she was a better person when she was with me.

When I asked her what made her want to pursue our relationship, she answered, "I saw your character, integrity, willingness to serve, generosity, and grit. I have never come across a person with your tenacity, determination, and inspiration." I share this with you not to impress you but to impress upon you that when you continue to work on yourself and gain the confidence to do what's necessary to reach your goals and dreams, you will undoubtedly make a comeback in your life! I went from the hurt I experienced in my prior relationship with a woman who could not weather the storm with me to feeling incredibly blessed with my **WIFE** of 8 years as of August 30th, 2022, with an overall 12-year relationship!

I'm so appreciative that we are in a great place, but I know 100% that the confidence I exude is contagious. My wife believes in me because of my willingness and ability to love intensely, and I attribute that to wanting to win. I don't know where you are with your confidence, but as you read this, you will soon understand what it will take to make a comeback in your life!

In my junior year in college, I did a presentation for a community service project I participated in for my Fraternity, Alpha Phi Alpha. When it was my turn to speak, I began to read the slides on the projector. Throughout the presentation, I continued reading. When I finished, I received a standing ovation; however, I knew I could have done better. My Fraternity brother, Ty Winston, pulled me to the side and was honest when he said to me, "That was not good." I accepted his feedback. I knew that I had to do something about it.

I found the motivational speaker, Les Brown, and acknowledged he was doing a Monday motivational call. I began to listen for several years, and I learned and observed his speaking style. On one particular Monday, a guest speaker, Andy Henriquez, was featured, and I was moved and inspired by his storytelling. I enjoyed Andy so much that I sought him out and hired him as my speaking and storytelling coach. That was a game changer that equipped me as a speaker and trainer!

Andy trained me for two years over the phone, and my skillset became impactful.

Andy was impressed with my speaking & storyteller skillset that he gave me an opportunity to speak at a personal development event in Fort Lauderdale, Florida, in 2014. This was my opportunity to reveal myself, and I did just that! Following my presentation, Andy pulled me over and said, "That was amazing!" He gave me great feedback. I asked myself what allowed me to make such an impact. I concluded that I developed confidence in my speaking and wanted to make a comeback. I also developed a confident spirit which made me a great speaker. This experience showed me the power of confidence and what you must do to get it.

Today, I take people step-by-step to develop their confidence and show them how they can make a comeback in their lives. The video was recorded in 2014, is on my website at www. thecombackexpert.com. So, when your confidence gets deflated and you need to be reminded that you have what it takes, I ask you to go to my website and watch how I made a comeback in my life and how you can do the same. I also have learned confidence is a superpower! Once you start believing in yourself, that's when the magic starts happening.

A strong' core' is the most important thing a person can have. The 'core' I'm referring to is being able to strengthen your mind, body, and soul regarding personal development, health-fitness-wellness, and spirituality. When a person is whole, it's rewarding as their confidence develops and grows stronger. However, it should be duly noted that strengthening or developing anything that has the potential to make you a better individual is an ongoing process. There is no endpoint!

While developing a strong core, I listened to personal development audiobooks, read books, and watched various videos from well-known thought leaders. In addition, I attended workshops and seminars to develop myself further. Regarding my health and fitness, I was committed to a set number of days per week to work out in the gym and receive additional specialty treatments for my recovery. I made sure to eat healthy and did not overindulge in foods that were not serving my overall needs. Spiritually, I worshipped in service, studied the bible, prayed, and served others. I also invested in self-care and personal time to recharge. I continue to exercise these disciplines today because I understand that development is ongoing, just like learning. I encourage you not to allow yourself to get to the place where you feel that you have 'arrived.'

As challenges were confronting me, I was able to make a comeback in my life because of the work I put into my 'core.' Each time I made a comeback, my confidence strengthened, and I began to overcome more of life's obstacles.

The purpose of this book is for you to develop YOUR process so that YOU can make a comeback and be 'core.' As you become 'core' you will become stronger and better equipped to handle life's situations. You will also be able to train yourself to make a comeback. It's refreshing to know that you have what it takes if you're willing to work! Jim Rohn says it best: "We must all suffer from one of two pains: The pain of discipline or the pain of regret. The difference is discipline weighs ounces while regret weighs tons."

I want you to be intentional about growing at the 'core' so that you are better equipped to overcome any obstacle in your life. That can only come with commitment and discipline to work on yourself daily. Time waits for no one, and as John C. Maxwell says, "A leader is always ready!" You will be ready to take on whatever adversity that knocks you down, and yes, you will be able to stand back up.

Les Brown – "If life knocks you down, try to land on your feet. Because if you can look up, you can get up." And if you can get up, you can stand up! Remember my story? That happened to me when I had my motorcycle accident. I ended up in a flower bed, and it took me 20 years to walk with my cane. If I can do it, whatever challenges you are facing today, you can overcome them. You must believe that you can do it.

Finally, I want you to take control of your thoughts and realize that the only thing that can hold you back is if you decide you don't have what it takes to succeed. So, decide you will take the necessary steps to build the confidence to make a comeback!

CHAPTER 5

"IT'S NOT WHAT HAPPENED TO YOU; IT'S HOW YOU RESPOND TO IT"

~Louis Moorer III~

"Persistence-the ability to keep moving forward, in spite of difficulties" – Byron Pulsifer.

At the beginning of dealing with any difficulty, responding to it is the LAST THING on someone's mind. We often REACT as opposed to responding. It's much easier to feel sorry for yourself or for the person that's dealing with any challenge. I have dealt with feelings of disappointment throughout my life. The one thing that kept me going was the ability to move on when things didn't work out the way I expected them to. Finally, I made the conscious decision to respond to what was happening to me. I saw that my situation had a far better outcome when I responded!

As I mentioned several times, beginning in Chapter one, I was involved in a motorcycle accident, which was a pivotal moment in my life. It happened six months after I turned 30 years of age. If I had not kept pushing forward, you would not be reading this book today. If I can make a comeback, so can you!

My motorcycle accident was the biggest defining moment in my life because there was so much uncertainty. So many voices were telling me things, but that little voice within always said to me, no matter what, keep pushing forward. In doing so, your greatest reward lies ahead. When I was in my late 20's, I ended a relationship that I knew wasn't serving me. Sometimes, I felt terrible, but I had to trust my instincts and move on. I even talked to my older sister, and she took me out and talked with me about life.

When we returned to my house, we sat in the parking lot, and she looked me in my eyes and said, "I know this breakup is hard for you, but you have to believe that your queen is out there." I held on to those words for years. Finally, however, I made a point to work on myself and develop myself so that when I met my queen, I would be the king (man) that I was supposed to be. A decade later, it happened because I chose to respond to my unfavorable situation and not react. It doesn't necessarily have to be love; it could be a job you're working for that you know is no longer serving you. Maybe it might be a health diagnosis or another serious issue that calls for a change in your daily habits. Whatever it is, you have to make a declaration to yourself that you have to understand, "It's not what happened; it's how you respond to it."

I witnessed many individuals take control of their lives and do the impossible. For example, my brother has a carpet cleaning business. Unfortunately, his partner of 5 years was going through some financial challenges and couldn't keep up with payments, leaving my brother with $33,000 in debt. Thankfully, my brother was also in real estate and ended up selling a few properties to settle the debt before the real estate recession of 2006.

The desire to have his own business kept him moving forward. That is how he chose to respond to his setback. Eight years later, he stayed the course and relocated to build the carpet business. In addition, he also is pursuing real estate again as an agent. Today, he sets himself apart from other carpet cleaning companies by offering satisfactory results, or the service is free. This would not have happened if he had given up when faced with adversity.

We all have a time in our life when we are tested. When tested, you have one decision: create a path of progression or retreat. In other words, you either get back up after being knocked down or stay down. You can train yourself when facing adversity. You can respond to the challenges with a positive, mental attitude because that's where the victory lies.

Being the comeback expert, I have accepted and been encouraged to keep pushing forward as a lifestyle. You may ask yourself, what does a pushing-forward lifestyle look like? A keep-pushing-forward lifestyle looks like continuing when you have setbacks, disappointments, and adversity. Once again, it's not what happens to you; it's how you respond to it that counts. You may not have any control over the above three, but you DO have the power over your mindset to keep pushing forward. That's where it begins and ends. When you get hit from the blindside, you cannot sit in sorrow and wait for people to come to your rescue. You must be willing to inoculate yourself from distractions and even interruptions from achieving your goal. Again, I ask you, is it easy? No, but is it worth it? Absolutely!

One of the most difficult challenges I faced was when I was scammed out of $15,000 from the ATM business. That was a lot of money! However, that incident didn't define me. Mark Twain – "I'm not a product of my circumstances; I'm a product of my decisions." I decided to become more business savvy and learn what to look for when making substantial business purchases. More importantly, I made sure to do my due diligence. Because I took that approach, I was able to recoup the $15,000 back tenfold. Recouping my $15,000 loss would not have happened if I had allowed the situation to paralyze me by having a negative reaction. But I chose to respond positively, and I encourage you to do the same.

Today, this book is a product of my speaking business. It would not have been a reality if I didn't put in the work and share with you how you can make great things in your life happen if you're willing to learn from your life lessons and do something positive and productive about it. As you do something about it, it's great for your mental health, your physical health, and your spirit.

It's great for your mental health because you won't allow yourself to go into a state of depression and feel like life is over. You will develop a confident spirit about yourself that will attract others, and you will understand that, as LC Robinson says, "In life, things will happen to you, things will happen around you, but what matters most is what happens inside you." Make it a point to equip yourself by reading books and having quality conversations with others who have been through trials and tribulations. Using their experience, they can assist you with responding to unfortunate circumstances.

It's great for physical health because you don't allow yourself to get stressed. Let me be clear! There is such a thing as good stress. In this particular case, I am referring to debilitating stress that prevents you from taking action to overcome whatever challenges you face. Working out (exercise) is a great way to relieve stress. Participating in whatever type of physical activity that gets your body moving and brings you joy is the key. Implementing physical exercise will assist in alleviating stressors that typically interrupt your ability to respond to adversity.

Lastly, it's great for your spirit. Scripture reminds us that in Philippians 3:14 – *I press on toward the goal to win the prize for which God has called me heavenward in Christ Jesus* (NIV). For me, my spirit comes from my faith. I am a God-fearing man who relies on the word to center and guide my path. I understand that not every individual who reads this may necessarily be a believer. I would humbly encourage you to find something that you can be inspired or enlightened by. Something positive that takes YOU out of the equation to provide you with a sense of purpose.

As I often push forward to respond to challenges, I acknowledge that I made it this far and it's a great feeling to know that the obstacles I was dealing with did not hold me back. Instead, I was able to motor through the challenges and gain a great sense of purpose. As stated in Chapter 1, I faced many obstacles as a child and grew more confident as I overcame each challenge. Next, I began speaking from a place of inspiration, hope, and motivation. My purpose became clear as I became an example for so many people. It forced me to work on my mindset, have a refreshing spirit, and operate with a positive attitude. Throughout it all, I became better, stronger, and wiser. I was being shaped and molded as an encourager.

Today, my sense of purpose has allowed me to impact so many people. You will acknowledge your sense of strength and perseverance by deciding to stand up and face your life challenges over time. During that process, I equipped myself as a better communicator. I could express how I felt and decided not to suppress my feelings. Being a great communicator, I could bond and connect with the right people to assist me with making a comeback in my life. Unfortunately, the people who equip themselves don't allow people to take advantage of them. They always get their needs met.

In 2007, I loaned $20,000 to a friend I had known for over 20 years. I wanted to be there for my friend; however, when it was time for repayment, I had to chase him down. I made phone calls at odd hours of the day and night. I continuously made follow-up calls, with no response on the other end. At that time, that was a defining moment for me. I could have easily taken my friend to court. I could have put his reputation on trial, but I decided to give it to God and let Him direct me on how I should handle this situation.

Because I looked to the Lord, I defined the moment by

being patient with this challenge. Finally, after eight long years, payments began to take place, and I was paid in full! What a blessing! I learned a valuable lesson in the process…Remember, it's not what happens to you; how you choose to respond to it makes the difference.

I often think about this incident, and I know I was continually equipping myself to become a great communicator during that time. However, I honestly believe if I hadn't worked so hard on myself, I would not have yielded the results I eventually ended up having.

It's not always easy when you decide to keep pushing forward. First, I had to understand what support really looked like. It's important to say that we all have busy lives; however, I found out what support looks like during one of the most extensive trials of my life. Before the motorcycle accident, I felt like I had a great support system of friends. However, when I lost my mobility, many people who were there for me began to disappear. I found out that the people who really cared about me would do things that were inconvenient and make a point to be there for me no matter what. I discovered that's the type of support you need in your life to keep pushing forward.

It's important not to block your blessings; however, that was not an option for me! I was on a quest to continue responding to life's hits and acknowledged that there were people who wanted to be there for me during this critical moment. It's important to discern who truly wants to be there for you and who wants to be nosey. I sincerely believe that the people who want to be there for you are your angels. Angels are a gift from God, and you should always cherish the angels in your life! In addition to angels, there are qualities you must have in order to keep pushing forward.

The first quality: Having a burning desire to rise above your circumstances. I have a burning desire to walk again without assistance. It will be 20 years as of July 5th. I have made many improvements, and I know it will happen for me, so I keep pushing forward. The second quality you must have is hope. Hope keeps the desire strong. When your hope is fulfilled daily, the task is not difficult. If you keep these two qualities in front of you as you push forward, it will inevitably happen for you!

If you want to make a comeback in your life, sitting still must not be an option. The qualities of having a burning desire and hope will fuel you every single day. Having hope is a fulfilling journey that makes your life even more extraordinary. People get inspired when they see a brighter future. So, I push forward and get excited about the process I experience.

As you have previously read, I met my wife online. During that time, I was getting older and wiser and was preparing myself for the man I knew I needed to become. I learned early on that my wife had a beautiful heart and believed in me. I wanted her to know that she made a great decision. However, I knew it would take time for us to bond and gel as a couple. So, I got excited about the process of us coming together as one. I was inspired every single day because my hope was powerful. But, I also knew I had to show her that I was a man of my word and that my actions speak for me.

As we grew closer and I knew she loved me, the hope I had

throughout the years prepared me to be the amazing husband God blessed me to become. As you continue reading, please pay close attention to that special 'something' that you're looking for. You must keep pushing forward until it becomes a reality.

Think of a time when you had hope, and it worked out in your favor. More than anything, you must allow yourself to have the imagination to take you to a place where hope is possible. In addition, having the ability and willingness to respond continuously to life's hardships will make all the difference in your life.

CHAPTER 6

"THE THRILL OF MAKING A COMEBACK"

~Louis Moorer III~

"My comeback was not about winning or losing; it was about the feeling of being able to compete at the top level again." – Steven Adler

There is such joy in bouncing back from life's obstacles. I say this because as I was riding my motorcycle and fell off, I broke my back and fractured my left arm. So much so that the bone protruded out of my skin. The doctor was unsure if I would gain full range of motion in my left arm again. During my recovery process, I needed to participate in ongoing occupational therapy. I worked several hours a day to regain the movement and function of my arm. I'm not saying it was easy, but it was worth it.

Today, I can use both arms to lift objects and ride motorcycles, and as I write this chapter, I am holding the pad and pen to formulate my thoughts—the thrill of deciding to stay on course no matter what has changed my life. As we deal with unforeseen circumstances and remain committed to staying the course, we experience joy and happiness. When joy and happiness take center stage in our lives, the thrills and emotions boost our inspiration and motivation. As I began to see and feel the progress in my life, it was (and still is) always exhilarating. The definition of a thrill is *a sudden feeling and excitement and pleasure.*

It was so exciting to take my first steps after being in a wheelchair for three months! As the tears came from my eyes, I was so overjoyed that the comeback was starting to happen. My belief was stronger than ever! I knew I could do this. Every day, I would see improvement. One day, I would begin to feel a new sensation in my legs. The next day, I would see my muscles developing. It's important to highlight that this process happens as we go through very challenging events. We have to gain control of where we are going to place our attention. I share this with you because you have the opportunity to understand that you can have thrills by overcoming what people may have said you couldn't. All you need is to believe and be a positive example for others.

I have found that throughout my recovery, being a positive example for others has been an additional layer of thrills in my life. So many people are hurting from the lack of belief, and they don't see the possibilities that their life can change. Having the faith to believe is essential when you make a comeback in your life. The people watching you will see your positive results. They want to see your joy and happiness and how you carry yourself throughout the challenge. When I learned this, I had to make peace with where I am and where I'm going. In other words, you may not be where you want to be today in life, but by striving to get there, you will see progress. Your ongoing progress should give you hope and faith that better days are ahead.

It pleases me when I see people make measurable progress. As a speaker, trainer, and coach, I have had clients who lacked the confidence and belief that they could do it. I immediately said, "Yes, you can!" I gave them stretch goals to get to the next level every day. They worked hard to improve, and I noticed their progress when we met for a follow-up session. It was thrilling for both of us (coach and client) that you can do better once you learn and know more. It brought us a great sense of satisfaction that they broke the spirit of the average person and committed to becoming better.

As this paradigm shift took place, results consistently happened in their lives. Because the thrill was so powerful, and the momentum of making life changes brought the best out of them. It's incredible what can happen when you keep the faith that your circumstance will improve. When going through life, people might say things to interrupt the thrill of making a comeback. Positive thinking is critical because you can't let anyone take your joy.

As I was making my comeback, it was said to me by my father that I won't walk. He was in the room talking to me, reciting what the doctors said. I know you may be thinking, wow, that's harsh coming from my own Father! However, I was wise enough to know that my father and the doctor were not in control. So, I focused on doing what I needed to do, such as rehabilitation, exercising my physical and mental fitness, and telling myself daily that this will work for me and I will walk again!!! I was willing to endure the pain and struggle of rehabilitation to achieve my ultimate goal of walking again. I was persistent and made no excuses. "Success is the progressive realization of a worthy ideal" – Earl Nightingale. My worthy ideal was walking again.

Success didn't happen for me overnight, but I believe because I stayed on course, I was able to make progress with my recovery. I often thought I would be so excited when I started walking again. I held on to that thought and feeling when I didn't feel like working out. When I didn't feel like reading my books, when I didn't feel like drinking water to hydrate my system, I imagined the thrill of making a comeback. If you're reading this book, you might be dealing with your own issues or circumstances and don't know what will take place. I want to assure you that if you continue to believe it can happen for you, it will happen! Yes, it will happen, but also know there's a thrill in making a comeback!

You are responsible for your success and happiness. To reach your full potential, you must do what's required to persevere and overcome what's holding you back. Once you acknowledge what's holding you back and deal with the fear, you will make small wins. The small wins will then turn into significant accomplishments. When I figured this out, I lived by the saying, "Take it day after day." I didn't just get through the day; I made each day count and set myself up for the day ahead. I knew what I would do the next day because I mapped out a schedule of events during my rehabilitation process. I took my rehabilitation one day at a time.

In order for any setback or life occurrence to give you a thrill, you have to put yourself in that place where you can see yourself rising above. So here's what I say to you as you read this book. Today is when you take control of your life and measure the small and the big wins. However, know that you have to appreciate the process and not apologize for wanting to celebrate your victories.

My wife bought her first car when she graduated from college. When she bought her car, she knew she had to be responsible. There were many times she had responsibilities that she had to take care of, and she shared with me in her words, "I'm strapped for cash." That was unique because I had never heard of that expression before. So we sat down and talked about ways she could pay her car off within the final year of the loan. We agreed that I would take care of the household bills for the year so that she could focus on paying her car note. I never wavered and stayed on course with my recovery.

Not only did my wife pay off her car loan, but we also enjoyed the feeling of achievement. I assisted her comeback with a great sense of fulfillment because she went from uncertainty to a game plan of knowing how she would execute paying off the loan. When she made her final payment, that experience was definitely a thrill and made her comeback much more meaningful.

Everyone has the ability to take ownership of their lives and put themselves in a better position. When doing so, the thrill of making a comeback fulfills your spirit and gives you a taste of success because you did something you thought was impossible.

So now, let's take on a new perspective when dealing with life's challenges and know there's joy and a sense of accomplishment when you execute your plan and do not quit. Allow this new perspective to play a vital role in how you view life, and know that there are thrills of satisfaction that will overwhelmingly consume you if you focus on what's important, which is to make a comeback in your life.

In addition, it's also important to note as your thrill of making a comeback begins; you have a feeling of passion that also fuels your journey. It was overwhelming when I took my first step because I had been in a wheelchair for over three months. However, it was promising, and my passion began to grow in a way that made me more excited about doing my daily exercises that would enhance the strength of my lower extremities. The definition of passion is a powerful emotion of love and hate. In this situation, I loved what I was experiencing. The thrill of making a comeback was amazing! The understanding of passion has helped me understand why I should love the joy of making a comeback.

Awareness gives understanding, and as you begin with the thrill of bouncing back, you must have the right attitude. The right attitude will assist you in whatever you must do to ensure you have the right state of mind to advance in the process. Learning from my Mother what love is, prepared me for what could have been a devastating experience.

As stated in an earlier chapter, when my house caught fire and I had to stay at a hotel with my girlfriend, she woke me up early that morning and told me that she couldn't be in this relationship with me anymore, then she left the room. At that moment, I knew I had to trust myself and do what was best for my life. I had to accept that there was no more passion or relationship. But, on the other hand, I had to get excited about my future and the thrill of (me) making a comeback and finding the true love of my life.

Sometimes things you can't control happen unexpectedly, and you must see yourself getting out of that situation. As long as you know that there are better days ahead and you see yourself where you want to be in life, allow the thrill of you making a comeback, keep yourself focused on what's important, and do not allow yourself to settle or feel depressed when things don't go your way. As long as you have passion in your life and know that there are thrills in making a comeback, it is NEVER impossible! Impossible means – I'm Possible! When you change the way you look at things, the things you look at change – Wayne Dyer.

CHAPTER 7

"WHAT DOES YOUR COMEBACK LOOK LIKE?"

~Louis Moorer III~

"The only time you should look back in life is to see how far you have come." – Kevin Hart

What does your comeback look like? That is a thought-provoking question for you to answer for yourself. Do you consider your comeback a test of your commitment to stay the course until achievement? I often wondered where I would be in a year if I put in the work required to achieve my life-changing comeback. As stated in Chapter 1, I'm still dealing with the life-changing setback of breaking my back. The prognosis at the time was not promising. Then, however, I visualized myself walking again. I kept that picture on my mind every day, without doubt of failure.

As you continue reading, you might be dealing with an injury or another kind of setback. I want you to think, what does your comeback look like? What will you do to achieve your victory? Without any sacrifice, there is no reward!!! I'm so thankful that I knew the importance of sacrificing what was required of me, such as eating healthy, drinking lots of water, exercising, and working on my mental fitness until my comeback started to happen for me. When dealing with a spinal cord injury, there is a lack of function in the body. The spinal cord is vital for all body functions because it is connected to the brain.

Because I injured my spinal cord, I lost the ability to urinate, and I had to wear a catheter for over six months. I still did everything I could during that time, such as exercise and drinking fluids for healing, but I also visualized myself standing up and urinating in the bathroom. Six months later, it finally happened. I was able to urinate independently without the use of the catheter. I attribute this to seeing (visualizing) myself being able to do this a year from now. I learned from this process it's essential to understand where you want to go and how making a comeback can happen for you. Many people have been told that making a comeback is impossible and that the probability for you is low. However, if you have seen anyone make a comeback or know someone who did it, that only means it can happen to you! Visualize and always begin with the results in mind.

Speaking from experience, I know you must know where you want to be and be willing to do everything possible to get there. In 2007, I went to Shanghai, China, to look into stem cell research. My prognosis – After receiving stem cell treatments, I could walk again without assistance. No wheelchair, no walker, no cane, just me standing and walking on my two feet! Can you imagine how happy I was when I heard those words? As a result, I spent 30 days in China, receiving six stem cell treatments. I thought every treatment would assist me with walking without any ambulation devices. Unfortunately, the treatments weren't effective. I invested $30,000 to help me walk again. Although it didn't work out the way I wanted it to, I could not and did not lose my joy. I stayed focused on where I wanted to see myself. And I always saw myself walking again.

When you face challenges in life, and you can visualize and see yourself making a comeback, and it doesn't happen the way you wanted it to, you can't get bitter, and you can't feel like it's impossible. It's crucial that you focus on where you see yourself going during the process of making a comeback. It may sound easy; however, that is necessary so that you don't allow yourself to give up. I didn't allow myself to give up after I lost $30,000 from undergoing six unsuccessful stem cell treatments when I traveled to China. Philippians 3:13-14 – *Brothers and sisters, I do not consider myself yet to have taken hold of it. But one thing I do: Forgetting what is behind and straining toward what is ahead, I press on toward the goal to win the prize for which God has called me heavenward in Christ Jesus.*" It would be best if you pressed on toward winning the prize by seeing yourself where you want to be. Visualizing accomplishment as you go through the process of what challenges you're dealing with makes your comeback journey very hopeful. Although I didn't walk out of the hospital in China with successful results from the stem cell treatments, I still visualized myself walking again because that's what my comeback looked like to me—walking – walking – walking again!

Your comeback can look however you want it to look as long as you're willing to put in the work to achieve the results that your heart desires. It might not happen overnight, and you may take years to achieve your goal, but you must see yourself crossing the finish line of accomplishment. As you use your imagination, you form a mental image of what could be despite it not manifesting in the physical sense, at least not yet. Imagination is vital in seeing yourself changing your current circumstances as you make a comeback in your life. The art of mental creativity or imagination sounds simple and easy to do. Yet, when negative feelings and emotions are involved, we allow our imagination to talk us out of doing what we need to accomplish our goals. Sometimes we don't FEEL like doing it when we know we SHOULD be doing it.

In the case of what your comeback looks like, now you know what is required to help you get to where you want to go, although you may not get there immediately. You know, however, what will sustain you when you can't see clearly ahead. This was imperative for me as I came back to the states from China, and I wasn't walking as the stem cell treatment team projected. Was I disappointed? Yes. Did I stop doing what I needed to do? No, because I let my imagination continue to drive me until tangible results appeared in my life. I had to master the art of discipline in order to stay the course of my daily exercise and rehab routine if I wanted to increase my odds of walking again. I kept a positive mental attitude that I would walk again.

I saw myself walking, and in order for me to walk, I had to be persistent and participate in daily activities such as strength training, aquatics, and stretching five days a week for years.

As I was working out, I saw myself walking because that was what my comeback looked like. I want to pause and ask you a question. Do you understand what your comeback looks like and what is required of you to achieve it? Now that you have thought it through, I want you to ask yourself, are you willing to do what's needed to achieve success?

The difference between making a vision come true or failing to achieve your goal is daydreaming. A daydream is a fantasy you have while you are awake. Daydreams can distract you from what's most important to you. On the other hand, a vision is a state of being able to see clearly. Therefore, it is more important to have a vision versus daydreaming. Throughout my journey, I have met many people who said they wanted to succeed. However, they talked as if they were daydreaming and were never really willing to stay committed to seeing their vision through.

I remember when I was in the pool working out during the earlier stages of my recovery when I was approached by someone who was watching me. The stranger said, "You are putting in the work with your workouts. It shocked me when the doctor told me that I would never walk again." He shared how I needed to work out several hours a day. After that, all I could think about was walking again, and my comeback could happen for me. All I had to do was stay committed to my process. This is the best example of using your imagination and focusing on what you want your comeback to look like.

Since then, I have also been an example for many people who are injured, overweight, or lacking confidence in themselves.

My questions for them are – How do you see yourself a year from now? And what does your comeback look like? As they reflect on their ideas and understand that imagination is important, they begin seeing (in their minds) the results they desire to accomplish and start putting in the work. I explained that visualization is the key! As John C. Maxwell says, "Dreams don't work unless you do." In other words, don't just dream the dream; work the dream! Be the person who knows what's required and is willing to do whatever you have to make that thought, that vision, become a reality.

In Stephen R. Covey's best-seller book – "*The 7 Habits of Highly Effective People,*" he says, "Begin with the end in mind." He asserts, "begin each day, task, or project with a clear vision of your desired direction and destination, and then continue by flexing your proactive muscles to make things happen." So many people start but don't see themselves finishing because they have no end in mind. So many businesses have started and failed because they quit and neglected to see the end in mind. I encourage you to start and finish with your end goal in mind.

When I was in my early 20s, I desired to have a clear complexion because I had acne-prone skin. I experienced this for years. I did everything possible, from listening to various aestheticians advising me not to eat fast food to not drinking sodas and avoiding refined carbohydrates. It was because I always kept the end in mind that I took heed and avoided those things. However, despite my efforts, I did not see the desired results, even though I was using high-end products. Then in

2010, I discovered the solution that changed my complexion: Clinically Clear!

The aestheticians at Clinically Clear were experts at caring for acne-prone skin for people of color. First, they did a thorough skin evaluation to determine my skincare needs. Next, the Clinically Clear experts provide me with personalized products and a specific regimen. I am still following their guidance and expert opinion to this day. I achieved the achieved results because I kept the end in mind. I also was focused on seeing what my comeback looked like. You now have examples of various comebacks I have made in my life. However, it's crucial always to envision what your comeback looks like for YOU.

Today, I get moved when people tell me I have a nice complexion. But, I also get constantly reminded when I hear it's imperative to stay the course until you accomplish what you want. Know where you want to see yourself despite how long it takes to achieve the end goal. Since then, I have inspired others who dealt with acne-prone skin. My mission was to empower them to take action so they could have a clear complexion. Those who were inspired have experienced similar results because they began with the end in mind. So, I want to pause here for a moment and ask you to take a hard look at your life and ask yourself: What's that special something in your life that you want to overcome, and how do you see that happening for you? Before it can happen, you must see yourself as victorious. This chapter was written (for you) to evaluate your adversities and, more importantly, look at how you would make your comeback, beginning with the end in mind.

In addition to knowing what you want to happen, how is your faith? What do you believe in? Do you believe in yourself? At age 30, when the doctors said I would never walk again, that was tough to accept. The one thing that kept me going was and is my faith. I knew that no man or woman could dictate my life. It was my faith and belief, and what I was willing to do to achieve walking again, is what was most important. Knowing these things, I was determined to walk again, and I did whatever I had to do to get out of that wheelchair. You're going to have to adopt the, no matter what, mindset when visualizing yourself getting to the next level. It will require tremendous energy and effort to get there while keeping the faith.

Byron King says, "If you argue with reality, you will suffer." The reality is faith is the one thing that we always look to because it gives us hope of the possibility of favor over something we have been striving to achieve. The greatest gift you can give yourself is vision. When you have the picture in your mind, it won't be as challenging to see yourself making a comeback because you will be able to see yourself and understand what your comeback looks like. You will do the things necessary every day because you keep the end in mind and let your faith guide you to accomplish what your heart and mind set out to do.

CHAPTER 8

"LEARN THE LESSONS IN MAKING A COMEBACK"

~Louis Moorer III~

The Dalai Lama says, "When you lose, don't lose the lesson." I have found great joy in losing because now I look for the lesson – WHY I DID NOT ACHIEVE THE GOAL! Learning the lessons should prevent you from making the same mistakes as long as you don't quit. Quitters never win, and winners never quit! You can't make a comeback if you quit when the going gets tough. Proverbs 24:10 (NKJV) – "If you faint in the day of adversity, your strength is small."

I often reflect on my biggest challenge that I'm still dealing with, which is my motorcycle accident. The lesson for me was/is to slow down. I was doing so much, and often, I was being reckless. I'm grateful that the good Lord spared my life on that fateful day. Despite that, I had to train myself to look at life's obstacles from a new perspective. I have experienced people immersed in self-help looking for better ways to use personal development to help themselves grow and prosper.

For many years, I was always taught to do the right thing and lead by example. In the mid-2000s, my brother and I built a large team for a network marketing company. Over time, we began to grow dissatisfied with the leadership. We made attempts to reach out to the leadership and express our frustrations. However, nothing was resolved. We, therefore, concluded that we could not lead our team by deception. Because of our fundamental differences, we talked to our team and let them know how we felt. We could no longer lead this team due to those differences. That was a pivotal point for me.

The lesson I learned was to lead, be authentic, and be genuine with my next leadership role and responsibility.

Today, I am a coach, and I often put myself in the shoes of other individuals (some are my clients) that I encounter. I take pride when working with challenging personalities or even people who are not motivated. I talk about what is required for them to reach the next level and remind myself that I must be a positive example for them.

The lesson is that when we have a team and create success, it's important to listen to everyone's perspective and find ways to meet in the middle that satisfies both parties. The key components I have learned that will build high trust and cooperation are transparency, trustworthiness, likeability, and consistency.

Experiencing the lack of leadership and unwillingness to do what's right fueled me to become the leader I am today. I know some people do not achieve their goals and dreams early on. Nonachievement may seem overwhelming; however, we must never forget if and when we lose, we must look for the lesson and not repeat the same mistake.

When you learn the lessons from different situations, you

will not only develop responses that will better equip you for success. You will gain valuable knowledge and experience to empower others. In addition, learning the lessons, instead of having the "woe is me" attitude, puts you in a leadership position.

This is important because you must learn from the experience when dealing with disappointment. This approach was vital for making a comeback when a leader I admired and thought highly of didn't do what was best for the team. Instead, he did what was best for HIMSELF. I can honestly say this is one of the reasons (why) I am a great leader. Humbly speaking, I do what I say I'm going to do because I never want anyone to feel or experience what I felt when my leadership disregarded our concerns.

This is one of the biggest reasons (why) I have made a comeback. I now look at life differently when things don't go how I want them to. Instead, I look at the lesson I'm learning from the experience. It has shaped and molded me to appreciate the process and use my life as a barometer of how I am growing and assisting others in developing.

In doing so, I have learned from previous challenges that I am able to gauge where I need to be or if more work is required. Similar to you, as you read this book, you can gauge from your own experiences whether or not you are where you need to be. This is one of the greatest lessons you could ever learn. So, when you're dealing with a setback and know that a comeback is required, you will automatically know the steps you need to take. However, if you don't know the steps (in making your comeback), I can help you with your action plan for achievement. My contact information can be found at the back of this book. Back to the story!

The lesson I have learned is that you have to be committed. You are in charge of staying the course in doing whatever it takes until you reach your victory. As I stated in this book, it's been 20 years since I've been on a quest to walk again, and it has not always been easy. However, my commitment to doing whatever it takes gives me the fuel to do what's necessary to maintain, sustain, and reach the point where I have advanced.

That's what it will take: when you face adversity, a positive mindset is required to motor through the challenge and learn the lesson. The growth does not come immediately, but it will over time. For example, when I was 16, I got my driver's license. I got a ticket about every other year for the past 40 years that I have been driving. In addition to that (don't laugh), I also got in other accidents. Throughout this process, I realized I was not learning from the lesson. I repeatedly attended traffic school, but yet and still, I would continue to get traffic tickets.

Finally, I learned (the lesson) that if I am patient with my driving and commit to following traffic rules, my reality of getting tickets would cease. It took me 35 years, but I learned the lesson. I share this with you because sometimes it may take a long time to get the lesson. The key is recognizing and acknowledging what needs to be done or stopped to see successful results.

Also, as I previously shared about my wife's desire to lose postpartum weight, she eventually learned that nutrition and exercise alone would not be as effective as they had been for her for so long. That realization came with trial and error from taking various approaches as she eventually incorporated intermittent fasting along with her nutrition and exercise. That was a game-changer for her. The goal of this section is for you to understand that there are lessons to be learned. More importantly, your commitment to learning the lesson is the key and prepares you internally to deal with the unexpected challenge that comes your way.

Not only did my wife try once, but several times until she learned that it was necessary to incorporate something in addition to what she was already doing to see the desired results. That's very similar to how we have to approach life. When the one thing we try isn't successful, we have to look at the lesson of why it didn't happen and what we can do better or differently.

Learning to master this skill will certainly demonstrate the ability to reflect internally, which will have a direct effect on your approach to your current adversity.

In learning from the lesson, I started to understand that habits are extremely important. I discovered that habits are essential to our health, which can make or break our choices of achieving and maintaining our lifestyle. Knowing that it is vital to develop duplicatable habits gives you a better chance of reaching the outcome that will serve you best. As you look at your life, it's important to acknowledge that you can live your life measured by the result of habits.

One bad habit is procrastination, not doing what you

say you are going to do when you say you are going to do it. Procrastination is the assassination of achievement and success. Using sophisticated excuses to promote poor habits does not serve your best interest. Instead, I encourage you to develop positive habits that benefit you. The type of habits that will give you positive results that you can repeat.

As I was recovering from my motorcycle accident (in the beginning), I lost my mobility in my lower extremities. I also experienced muscle loss or also known as atrophy, from not being able to work out at the intensity level that I had always been accustomed to. That was a major transition for me because, before my accident, I was extremely active, and now I had to rebuild my foundation. I sat and thought about what could I do since I lost my mobility to move and used what I found as a lesson in overcoming this challenge. I learned that I still needed to incorporate physical fitness in order to rebuild what I had lost, as that would ultimately improve my overall recovery from my motorcycle accident.

I made a habit of working out five days a week. Although I lost my strength in my lower extremities, I developed good habits because of the lessons learned. Habits are contagious and can help you motor through any adversity you face to help you get through whatever challenge lies before you. However, there are lessons to be learned from developing and using good habits that can help you recover from the trials and tribulations you're dealing with.

My wife helped me understand that health is important, not just working out. There were times when I would exercise, but then I wouldn't fuel my body with the proper nutrients necessary for optimal health.

When she told me this, I really started to pay attention to her life and how she ate. I saw that she was serious about her health, and I watched what she ate. That made me look closer at my life and acknowledge that what I was putting in my body was not helping me. Because of my wife's good healthy eating habits, I started using the health supplement line of products. As a result, I can attest to significantly changing my overall health and wellness.

I contribute to the change in my health and wellness by forming healthy eating habits (like my wife) and maintaining those habits. But, despite it all, the habits you develop will either help you or hinder your progress in making a comeback.

In order to get the best results, it's important to look for the lesson in adversity. Yes, it is about winning, but you can learn when you lose. You can learn so many lessons about your life if you adopt the mindset that when you lose, don't lose the lesson! I've been fortunate to change my life and the lives of so many others because we focus on what we have learned.

When my wife and I were engaged, we wanted to make sure we had established a spiritual foundation. We joined a church, and in doing so, we became excited and knew that we had a lot of talents and gifts to offer. We intentionally spoke with our pastor about leadership and how we wanted to be involved. For months, we waited patiently for a response on how to utilize us best. Unfortunately, no one ever followed up with us! We started to understand that people say things that can strike an emotional chord and make you feel wanted. But when it comes to communication and feeling involved, it was never a priority. My wife and I shared our feelings of neglect and disappointment that no one had followed up with us.

We were at a point when we were not appreciated, and something from then on had to be changed on our part. So we prayed long and hard and realized that although we loved the church family, we needed to seek a new church home.

We're thankful (to this day) we followed our hearts because we found another church that embraced, nurtured, and undergirded us as babes in Christ and welcomed our gifts and talents. Because we were not afraid to step out on faith, my wife and I were appointed to facilitate a six-month workshop for married couples titled "Kingdom Marriage." We were blessed to have the assistance of a seasoned church member and supporting material from Tony Evans.

We learned that when you're not being appreciated, step out on faith and go where you can grow. In life, there will be times when you experience opportunities to learn lessons, and it's your responsibility to change the things that you can from each lesson learned. In everything we do, when you lose, don't lose the lesson. Albert Einstein – "The definition of insanity is doing the same thing over and over and expecting different results." If we do not learn from our lessons, we repeat them.

I want to leave you with the understanding that the lessons you learn develop good habits. You will realize that some habits will serve your best interest and others will not. As I stated earlier, in making a comeback in my life, I developed habits that brought out the best in me and fueled my desire, creating a situation that was considered impossible possible. I learned that some habits will guide us or misguide us toward what we need to become that ultimate champion. Having a strong sense of discernment will aid in minimizing the habits that don't necessarily serve you.

Today, you can start creating new habits by asking yourself how these habits will serve me. What do I need to change? For example, suppose the habits help to improve my spirit, finances, overall health, goals, or relationships. In that case, I can automatically presume that any other habits would not serve me well if it gets in the way or robs me of my full potential. So, as you read on, it would be best to acknowledge whether or not the habits you have, serve you. In the words of the Dalai Lama –*"When you lose, don't lose the lesson."*

CHAPTER 9

"WINNERS NEVER QUIT; QUITTERS NEVER WIN (DON'T QUIT)!"

~Louis Moorer III~

Charles Allen – "When you say a person or a situation is hopeless, you're slamming the door in the face of God." Facing a trial is never easy. Often, you will question yourself. For example, at the beginning of recovering from my motorcycle accident, I was going through so many different emotions. I wondered if I would ever walk again. I wondered if I would ever play sports again. Would I ever be able to pick up my children and my wife? Will people look at me or treat me differently?

While in need of a wheelchair, I fantasized about how life would be when I began using a walker. Then, finally, I did the work to achieve the mission. I had multiple therapy sessions during my rehabilitation journey—Aquatic Therapy, Occupational Therapy, and Physical Therapy, to name a few. I saw the progress and felt ongoing improvement. My motivation was to score a 10 to get to my next level. In my case, the next level was for me to be able to walk with a quad cane. My confidence continued to strengthen, and I had moments when I would be so grateful that I didn't quit.

In the beginning, (to be honest), I had so much uncertainty about whether the therapy sessions would benefit my recovery. I had a personal goal set with a timeframe that was not aligned with my therapists' goals. It was discouraging at first; however, over time, I began to see how my body and nervous system responded to my efforts in my therapy sessions. My vision became so crystal clear about where I was going. More importantly, the strength in my legs was constantly improving. I began walking with a single cane because I didn't quit!

Thomas Edison – "Many of life failures are experienced by people who did not realize how close they were to success when they gave up." During uncertain times, my faith kicked in, and because of the strength of my faith, I was creating my future. I attribute success to God because He is the source of my life. He never quit on me, and I never quit on myself.

It's never easy facing life occurrences, and when you do, how do you continue without feeling you can't make it? Simply put, don't quit! Is it easy? No, but is it worth it? Absolutely! Just as I had faith in my recovery, I have faith in you and what you can achieve in your life!

In 2004, I began my network marketing career. I was an independent contractor with Legal Shield (AKA, Pre-Paid Legal). Empowering people to know their legal rights was rewarding as a representative. However, I did see many people start the business but wouldn't be there several months later. I found out the attrition rate for a network marketer is six to eight months. I didn't want that to be my reality, so I worked the business. As I worked in the business, I grew in rankings, was able to interact with leaders of the company, and made it to executive director. I was privileged to be a part of meetings with the company's leaders.

One of the leaders said: "Louis, it's impossible to stop a man or a woman who will not quit." He knew I was faced with the challenge of recovering from a motorcycle accident while also trying to start a business. To this day, that quote still rings true! It is so easy to want to throw in the towel when you get knocked down by life. But, in those moments, you must dig deep within yourself and know that what you are going through is just a phase and not a way of life. So, as you continue reading, you might be moved by that quote. My response is: Don't just be moved by the quote, but work the quote into your life because quitters never win, and winners never quit! Learning never to quit is a process. It's important to take one challenge at a time and as the challenge gets more difficult, learn how to persevere until you overcome it. In other words, you might need to take the necessary steps until you finally achieve success.

One of my favorite sports is basketball, a game about momentum. There is a time when one team builds momentum and the other team losses momentum. As I watch my favorite team play (the Golden State Warriors), they might be playing from behind because the opposing team has momentum in their favor. However, as the game continues, the Warriors take the lead. They played like this for years; however, it wasn't always that way. The Golden State Warriors had to learn how to win and create momentum. This is an excellent illustration of how you must remember never to quit, whether the momentum is on your side or not.

Life is about momentum. You are constantly learning how to win, but along the way, challenges will occur. When challenges occur, can you take steps to get the momentum back on your side, or will you quit? You may be thinking, what kind of steps do I need to take to win? First, it starts with having a positive mental attitude and adopting the I can, and I will do it mindset. These are two of the many crucial steps toward achievement. You are already defeated without having the I can, and I will do it mentality. Finally, enjoy the process until you are victorious.

It's important to share with you that many of the people we admire and hold near and dear to us are people who didn't quit. Dr. Martin Luther King Jr., a revered icon, was instrumental in the Civil Rights Movement, which began in 1954 and ended in 1968. There was so much segregation and people of color being taken advantage of. Yet, through it all, Dr. Martin Luther King Jr. remained positive and hopeful that one day people of color would share equal rights with their European counterparts.

It took 14 years to see positive changes within the judicial system that acknowledged and granted equal rights to people of color. Although this was the foundation and the outcome improved, today, as we live in the 21st century, there are still issues that people of color are still fighting for regarding Civil Rights. Black Lives Matter has become a new mantra that people of color have adopted and rallied for in the wake of the Civil Right Movement.

We are thankful that the Civil Rights Movement has shown us how having a positive attitude and never quitting made changes, and that's why we have the freedoms and rights that we do today. Although we have transitioned to the Black Lives Matter movement, due to the unjust killings of people of color by law enforcement, we will not quit. Until racial injustice is recognized and resolved, we continue to rally and protest peacefully.

In addition to Dr. Martin Luther King Jr. being a prominent leader of the Civil Rights Movement, he was also a brother of Alpha Phi Alpha, a fraternity founded in 1906. Its mission was about manly deeds, scholarships, and love for all humanity. Like Dr. King, I also went through the rigorous process of becoming a Historic Alpha Phi Alpha Fraternity member and brother. I must admit, it wasn't easy. There were times when I wanted to quit. I was reminded of all the greatness that came before me and how greatness showed up today. That history kept me going. I completed becoming a brother of the Alpha Phi Alpha Fraternity in July of 1995.

I'm so appreciative that I endured the process until the end and was able to create results in my life like the many prominent frat brothers who came before me. All because we all didn't quit!

It's becoming obvious to me that people who get ahead in life make a declaration to themselves that no matter what, quitting is not an option.

I often sit in my office and wonder why people choose to operate from a lack of desire. Being The Comeback Expert, I personally inspire people to do their best, and whenever I witness looks of despair, I turn them into hope and motivation to never quit. You ALWAYS have a choice to make! The choice I have mastered since knowing that comebacks are possible is to always do what is required.

I have always admired how my wife communicates and has the ability to teach, particularly with the youth. She is articulate and knowledgeable on most subjects and has often sought assistance to work with students. I remember asking her, "Honey, were you always a good student?" She replied, "Not always, especially in college." My wife attended Cal State University Sacramento at the time. She was transparent about her struggle to pass Organic Chemistry. Her major was Kinesiology. She expressed being at a crossroad because she thought Kinesiology may not have been the right major for her. However, she knew she had come too far with her courses to start over.

My wife decided to repeat the course and stick it out to the end. I asked her what she did differently to ensure she passed Organic Chemistry the second time. She asserted, "First, I got over my pride and began to sit towards the front of the class (where there were fewer distractions)! Second, as the semester progressed, I befriended a group of classmates who were getting A's and B's in the course, and they agreed to have study groups outside of class. Whenever they could not meet, I sought a tutor to assist me with my studies."

Needless to say, not only did my wife pass the course, she graduated with a Bachelor of Science in Kinesiology and has been tutoring young students in her spare time to this day!

When I asked my wife why she tutors after all these years, she responded, "Because I know how it feels not to understand the content and suffer in silence by not asking for help in class. So many students have felt like that. So I pride myself as that 'lifeline' to help them with whatever subject challenges them."

My wife made a decision not to quit and made a comeback with her studies, and she was also an example in her own life. I know when there are setbacks and challenges in her life, she's able to draw upon the times when it was difficult, but she DID NOT QUIT!

Here's what I say to you: There are going to be times in your life when you have to draw upon a life occurrence and reflect on what got you through. I know if you choose to operate from this place, there's going to be nothing that you won't be able to make a comeback from. So often, I receive comments from people saying; if I had the strength and discipline, I could lose weight. I can budget my bills. I can have a relationship like yours. But I can honestly say it's not that easy. There are challenges with all of those situations. Yet, I refuse not to quit but equip myself to be better, stronger, and wiser. So, in my mind, quitting is never an option!

When I was a little boy, my coach always said, "How bad do you want it?" whenever he was conditioning us into physical shape. As I ran up and down the court, I often said that to myself. I learned that when you're going through life, you have to give yourself pep talks. Doing so gives you the motivation and the will to win. Today, I constantly give myself pep talks. When faced with a challenge, I must control my mood and not let self-doubt seep into my thinking and talk me out of it. I constantly tell myself I can, yes, I will.

It doesn't matter where you are. It matters where you're going. Keeping that train of thought has always propelled me to where I wanted to go. It has allowed me not to quit on myself and be the winner I am today to change and impact lives.

As you continue reading this chapter, here is my coaching challenge: never quit, no matter what. If you quit, you will live a life of regret. For you not to live a life of regret, your call to action is COMMITMENT! Being committed to the cause is essential for achieving success. What I mean by that is that you stay the course no matter what until victory takes place. So, commitment is your call to action!

One of the most incredible life experiences I held on to was staying committed to the cause when I was expelled from school. Unfortunately, that journey set me back, and I was placed in remedial classes for several years. However, as I often look back, I have risen to a higher level of intellect because I was able to advance from those remedial classes and never gave up, no matter what. Throughout the journey, I was tested by both family and friends. But, more importantly, it gave me a perspective on life in spite of the opposition to never conform to the status quo.

CHAPTER 10

"YOUR CALL TO ACTION"

~Louis Moorer III~

How have we started something because we were fired up initially but didn't finish it? Have you ever stopped to ask yourself why? Often enough, it comes down to emotion. What may have initially drove us or motivated us to start was not strong enough to see it through. I have learned that motivation will only get you so far in life because emotion will always sway your desire to finish. You can't let your emotions (feelings) dictate your success or failure. What's important to understand is that it takes discipline to reach your goals and finish what you start. The definition of discipline is doing the thing you said you were going to do long after the feeling has left you.

My Godfather used to tell me as a kid, "If you discipline yourself, no one else will ever have to." At that time, I always thought of that as a profound statement! However, as I look at life now, I see that many people have to be disciplined. There's a reason why people go to the doctor and get diagnosed with unknown health conditions. One may argue that a lack of discipline may have played a significant role in the outcome. There's a reason why some people live beyond their means and find themselves in insurmountable debt and are struggling to repay it. Again, one may argue that a lack of discipline may have impacted their negative financial outcome. There's a reason why some people are unsuccessful in relationships of any kind. A lack of discipline and not using the how to win friends and influence people principles may have played a role in the outcome.

As you can see, there is a recurring theme here of what happens when discipline is not exercised on a consistent basis. In making a comeback in your life, this book outlines the philosophies as well as what's required for you to make a comeback in your life. I must add there are action steps that you must follow. Personal development is necessary! It allows you (and me) to grow at the core so you can feel good about yourself as you face adversity when overcoming challenges.

Throughout the years, growth has taken place in my life, giving me the consciousness to keep moving forward because my mindset has expanded exponentially. When dealing with adversity, your mindset will develop because you are trying to figure out a way to overcome it. Oliver Wendell Holmes Jr. says, "A mind that is stretched by a new experience can never go back to its old dimensions." When you are dealing with a life-altering situation, your mind is forced to stretch, and you have to grow. Once you have stretched your mind, it will never return back to the way it was unless you choose to allow it. This comes in the form of self-sabotage, negative self-talk, and limited or stinking thinking.

I had to implement this when doctors told me I would never walk again. He spoke to me from a medical perspective, and

I appreciated his advice. But I knew there were other people with severe challenges that accomplished what seemed to be impossible because they made their comeback possible. They knew others had done it, and they knew that they could do it too. So, by dealing with your life experiences, you will become better equipped to handle life's challenges in a way that allows you to rise above your circumstances. If one chooses to apply limiting beliefs, that will be the exact type of result one will receive – limited results.

You are forced to take action when you internalize what you read and experience. The action steps for you to take may be to make that difficult decision. It may be to make that call, and it may be to make changes to your health and quality of life. It may be hard to have the tough conversation with someone. But, on the other hand, it may be simple to take that leap of faith! Knowing all of this, we know that action is required, but it's up to us to do the necessary activities so that we can have the results that we want.

Throughout this journey, I have intentionally been building myself into the person that I need to become. I invested in personal development by reading books, listening to audiobooks and other positive content, attending seminars, and engaging in conversations with like-minded individuals to elevate my spirit and motivate me to level up with goals and dreams. These have profoundly changed the way I view myself and my abilities despite what the eye can see and what the naysayers attempt to put on my spirit. I believe wholeheartedly that I would not be the person that I am today had I not made the decision to put my comeback expert mindset into action. We all are work in progress, and I don't believe I have arrived. As long as there are goals and aspirations to achieve, there will always be some form of action that will be vital to seeing them come to fruition.

I also believe that we owe it to ourselves to make a comeback. Far too many sacrifices have been made before we can live a better life. It saddens me when I see people who are not applying themselves and don't have a burning desire to achieve more. Instead, they moan and groan and complain when things are not going their way. However, if the finger is pointed back at themselves, they would realize they are in control. So, instead of moaning and groaning, they must take action. It's a blessing to have others like family, friends, or mentors pour into you and speak life into your spirit. But it's all for nothing if you don't take action or exert effort. So, you owe it to yourself to make the decision to be intentional at rising above the situation that you are dealing with. Your call to action can be to make a comeback with the challenge you're facing. It's essential to take a realistic look at your life and be willing to make the adjustments needed to get ahead.

As I start to take a realistic look at my life, I acknowledge the areas where I need to become stronger. It was always easier to get ahead because I always did something to strengthen the areas where I was weak. If it's with my health, physical fitness, nutrition, or intellect, I acknowledged I had to equip myself with more information, so I didn't feel limited. I have seen when people are not willing to take ownership of their shortcomings and fall prey to getting taken advantage of.

Your call to action: be deliberate about what you want and where you want to go in life. More importantly, you must be deliberate about what action steps are required to get there. It's time to stop dancing around your shortcomings and put yourself in an environment where you will be supported and excel at making a comeback in your life. However, I'm still on the quest of walking without assistance, and now I use a cane to help me get around. I constantly grow at the core and align myself with people who can help me reach the next level. The next level for you is to decide to align yourself with the people in your life that can assist you with living out your goals and dreams.

So don't take this call to action lightly. Make that declaration to yourself that I'm going to get there. I'm going to get there because I'm not going to lean on my own understanding but rather allow the patterns of success to assist me with making a comeback in the areas where I'm not strong. Unfortunately, many people may not be willing to do that because the idea of being comfortable will prevent them from stretching to grow. As I have mentioned before, anything in life worth having will not be easy to obtain, which is precisely why it is so rewarding when one has reached their goal. That's what sets an individual apart from just thinking about doing something and actually doing it!

It's incredible how we can be quick to advocate and take action for other people and causes without anyone trying to motivate or encourage us to do all we can. Yet, when it comes to ourselves and wanting to get to the next level, we often shy away or shrink in our thinking when acknowledging what action steps will be necessary to see our goal or overcome our adversity. If I may, I'd like to be transparent, and please know it comes from a place of sincerity. If you continue to do the things you have always done, you will continue to see the same results!

About a year ago, my wife expressed her desire to acquire a notary commission and complete a general and specialized course for loan signings within the real estate arena. Naturally, I wanted to support her, yet, I also asked her how she would manage to meet all the demanding needs while caring for our young daughter, who required full-time general and medical care. She simply said: "I will find a way."

I have always known my wife to be determined to accomplish anything she sets her mind to achieving. So, when I say to you, she figured it out, she did just that! Her reason for pursuing this opportunity was to become her own boss. Being her own boss allowed her the flexibility to dictate her schedule, create a list of services, and decide what fees were appropriate to charge her clients. In addition, being her own boss would ultimately allow her to be home for our family without asking anyone for permission.

My wife realized the action steps she needed to take would have to coincide with our schedules so I could relieve her for breaks in order for her to study. My wife used her study time when our daughter was napping and late at night after our daughter was sleeping. After I went to bed, my wife could study to pass the courses and the state exam. Was it easy to do those things in addition to the extraordinary responsibilities of a wife and mother? No, but did she talk herself out of doing it? No. Her reason 'why' was bigger than any excuses she could have given not to pursue the opportunity she said she wanted.

She didn't allow the challenges of motherhood, taking care of a family, and nurturing our marriage to stop her from achieving her end goal. It was a journey for both of us! I couldn't have been prouder when she shared (with me) that she had passed the state exam and loan signing exam. She decided to achieve her goal, and she did. My wife is an excellent example of using discipline, commitment, and taking action, as she empowered herself to achieve her goal. My wife often tells me how I inspire her, but I am not ashamed to express to her just how much she inspires me too!

If you want to overcome a challenge in your life or take an area of your life to the next level, first you must make the decision to be committed and have the discipline to identify and execute whatever action is necessary to achieve it. I believe in you, and you should believe in yourself! You have the potential to achieve anything you want in life. You have the tenacity (inside of you) to make a comeback if you have faith and do the work required.

I sincerely hope I inspired and motivated you to take whatever action you need to in your life to overcome whatever hardship you are facing or to reach whatever goal you have set for yourself. No one else is going to make the decision for you. It is entirely up to you. If you need an accountability partner to assist you with staying on track, by all means, take advantage of that. If you need to invest in personal development or hire a coach, or mentor, do it. Once you realize that it will benefit you, you will better understand why the path along your journey looks the way it does. So, whatever call to action you feel you need to take in your life, I highly encourage you to take it!

After reading the previous chapters, hopefully, you now have a much better understanding of what's required of you to overcome the challenges that will come into your life. So, please take a moment to recall a time in your life when you successfully faced a challenge and turned it into a favorable result. What were those achievement steps? How long did it take for the situation to turn around? How long did you find your moment of clarity and discover your power within? How long did it take for you to harness your power of purpose?

Looking back, I remember when I had a timeline goal to be walking, and I, unfortunately, didn't reach the goal. However, I stayed the course by developing and strengthening my mindset as I continued to weather the storm. The call of action for me was: NEVER GIVE UP! As we go through life, we're going to have goals and set dates, and when it doesn't happen, you can't quit. You may have to pivot, but you can't quit. You might stop, step back, reaccess where you are, and then continue. As long as you never quit, you can moove forward. These are the times when you have to reflect on your call to action that you have learned throughout your life and apply it.

One of the most important things you can remember is to discipline yourself so that no one else will ever have to. As stated earlier, my Godfather shared this with me repeatedly so I could succeed in life. I took this approach to be structured and disciplined to get the results in my life that I was seeking. What was the call of action you learned that has been instrumental in transforming your life? How did that paradigm shift propel you to take action? I elaborated on discipline because that has been vital for me in making comebacks. I did not do it once or twice; I made a comeback repeatedly until I reached my goal. In order for you to win in the game of life, you are going to have to be disciplined. It's not a bad thing; discipline rewards you for consistently manifesting your dreams.

In addition, discipline is undoubtedly helpful to implement what you may not even be aware of as to what has already helped you thus far in being victorious regarding conquering adversity. When facing opposition, I had to reflect on the call to action that would help me get through the challenge and apply the philosophies as well as the disciplines to assist me with conquering my trials. You are now better equipped, dig deep within your mind and find a way to reach your mountain top!

CONCLUSION

The real glory is being knocked down to your knees and then making a coming back. Vince Lombardi – That's real glory; that's the essence of it."

In writing this book, my mission was to gather my thoughts and experiences from making a comeback in life in hopes that they will inspire you to push through when circumstances seem impossible to overcome. Throughout my journey, I witnessed so many people giving up on themselves. By telling my story, if I can motivate, inspire and give hope to others, they too can make a comeback in their lives.

Writing this book was fulfilling for me on various levels. In life, there are so many challenges that people are dealing with. Hopefully, by now, you have gained a few takeaways and know how to apply them to your own life. You never know how much you can inspire others by staying the course and seeing things through! Although I don't memorize quotes because they sound good, I take great pride in living by the quotes and philosophies shared throughout this book so that I can handle challenges.

I want to close as I opened: In life, you're going to get hit, and it's going to be unexpected. However, when life knocks you down, if you apply this to your life, there's not a comeback that you cannot make!

So, I am leaving you with the thought process that I have adapted when making a comeback is necessary.

The mission from now on in your life's journey is to implement the following list whenever life knocks you down:

1) **CONFIDENT SPIRIT** – The belief that no matter what comes your way or sets you back, you have what it takes to turn it around and make a comeback. I applied this when the doctor told me I would never walk again. I held onto that when things didn't go my way. I experienced setbacks and knew I had to remain confident that this would pass. Because of being confident, I was able to write this book. My mission is to let you know that it can happen to you as long as you don't let your confidence waver. What results are you looking for?

2) **BE COMMITTED TO THE CAUSE** – Continue to show up while in the midst of your adversity. No matter how it looks, continue to put your head down and do the work to see the desired results. Staying committed to the cause will always help you advance when dealing with making a comeback. When you quit, it's over, but if you remain committed to the cause, things will start to happen for you! What commitments are you willing to make?

3) **MAKE HAVING A COMEBACK A PART OF YOUR LIFESTYLE**

In order to make a comeback in your life, you are required to adopt the previously mentioned antidotes into your daily life, habits, and thoughts process. This will equip you immensely to get up after you've been hit by life! Knowing that you will deal with adversity makes this a lifestyle that will continuously inspire you to take action when you get hit by life's hard knocks. What habits will you develop that will empower you to make a comeback and become a part of your lifestyle?

4) **DEVELOP A WINNING MINDSET** – Knowing that you will come out victorious before adversity even presents itself. From the start, you cannot win if you are already defeated in your mind. Tell yourself, and, more importantly, believe that you have more than what it takes to win! You may have to pivot, but don't leave room to quit! Furthermore, having a winning mindset will always get you through life's uncertainties. What part of your thought process must you change to have a winning attitude or mindset?

Zig Ziglar – "You don't have to be great to start, but you have to start to be great!" It's true! You have to start somewhere, and the list provided is a foundation of what will help you navigate through life's trials and tribulations. Don't expect perfection early on. You will master it over time, and with trial and error, you will achieve. The ultimate point is to learn how to utilize your trials and errors as you see fit and apply those lessons in your situation when warranted.

Let your comeback begin!

FINAL NOTE BY THE COMEBACK EXPERT

While going through the process of becoming a published author, on October 6th, 2022, my father passed away from this earthly life as we know it. However, I have never experienced the loss of a parent, as my mother is alive and well. Speaking of being the comeback expert, this is one comeback that I must deal with for the remainder of my life.

From this experience, I will be able to sincerely speak to those of you who have lost a loved one. As we wake up every day after the loss of a parent or loved one, we are also expected to continue pressing on with making comeback, after comeback, after comeback.

Any excuse is a reason to fail! As I pay my respects and honor my earthly father, I know my heavenly father would not burden me with something that I could not handle, like my motorcycle accident, my 20-year comeback journey to walk again, and now, the loss of my earthly father. This short story is another example of facing challenges head-on, even when their origin blindsides us. It's not what happens to us; how we deal with what happens to us is the critical key to unlocking life, liberty, and the pursuit of happiness.

Writing this book, having weekly meetings with my coach,

being a husband, father, and son, supporting my family during my father's homegoing calling from the heavenly father, and dealing with my own challenges did not allow me to make excuses as to why I did not finish writing this book. But that is the true essence and meaning of the title of this book: – Don't Let The Cain Fool You: How To Make A Comeback From Ant Adversity, is all about.

BREAKING NEWS: It's Time To Get Serious by Finding Your Moment of Clarity, harnessing your power of Purpose, and allowing nothing to hold you back from making the comeback you deserve!

Louis Moorer III
Don't Let The Cane Fool You
How To Make A Comeback From Any Adversity
The Comeback Expert

ABOUT THE AUTHOR

Louis Moorer III is a strategic storytelling expert, speaker, and coach who has the unique gift of creating, perfecting, and delivering transformational messages that leave a lasting impact on his audience. His spellbinding delivery style, powerful content, and story transparency are why he branded himself as "The Comeback Expert."

Whether on stage and captivating an audience with his heartfelt and compelling message or facilitating workshops and training, Louis' impact resonates with audiences from all walks of life. His personal experiences and accomplishments are diverse and vast, giving him a unique ability to relate to all audiences.

Louis was born to hard-working parents who did everything possible to support their son's goals and dreams while instilling core values (in him) that would serve him later in life. Values such as hard work, discipline, commitment, and perseverance allowed Louis to surpass limiting expectations others had of him. At an early age, Louis attended and graduated from San Jose State University. Louis has served his community as a Social Worker for over 17 years and shares his personal story when the opportunity presents itself.

Louis enjoys the industry of Social Work, and he has also answered the call and purpose to become an entrepreneur, speaker, and coach by taking others by the hand and showing them how they, too, can make a comeback in their own lives.

Louis is known for delivering messages that go beyond the mind and penetrate the hearts and spirits of audiences. A sought-after speaker and trainer, he has spoken to various audiences, from the youth to ministry, non-profit, and personal development seminar audiences.

To learn more about Louis, his products, and coaching services, visit him at www.thecomebackexpert.com.

PICTORIAL SECTION

motorcycle accident

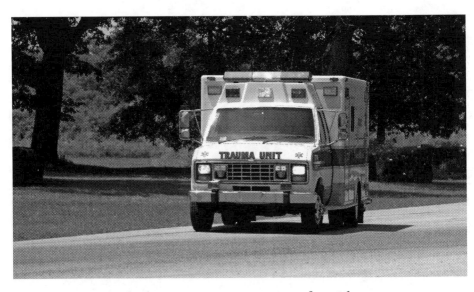

ambulance coming to scene of accident

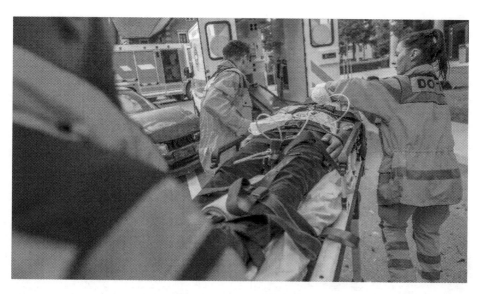

paramedics transporting Louis on
gurney going into ambulance

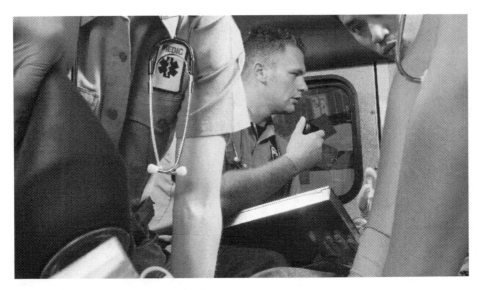

Louis in ambulance receiving emergency
medical treatment at scene of accident

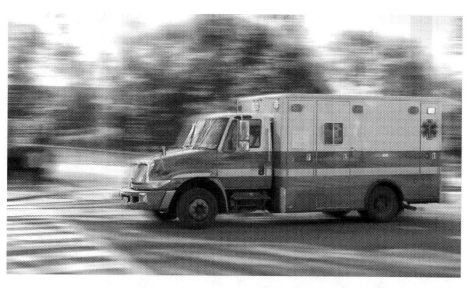

Ambulance rushing to the hospital with Louis

Ambulance arriving at hospital
emergency entrance with Louis

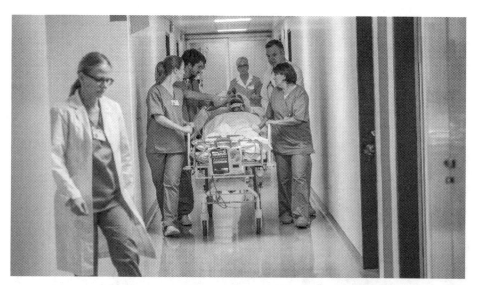

Doctors wheeling Louis to operating room on a stretcher

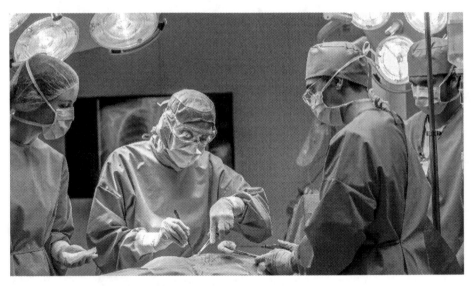

Louis is having surgery in the operating room

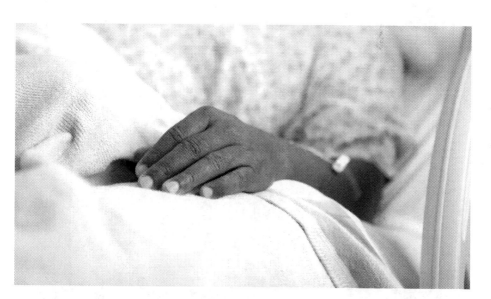

Louis in the recovery room after surgery

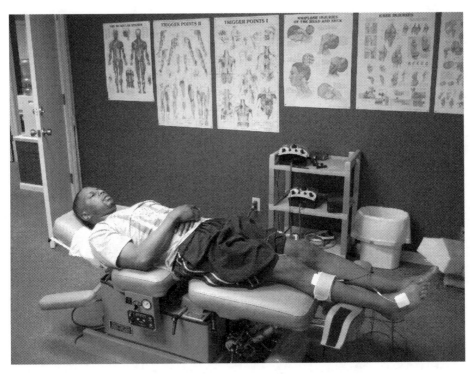

Louis In rehab in San Jose California

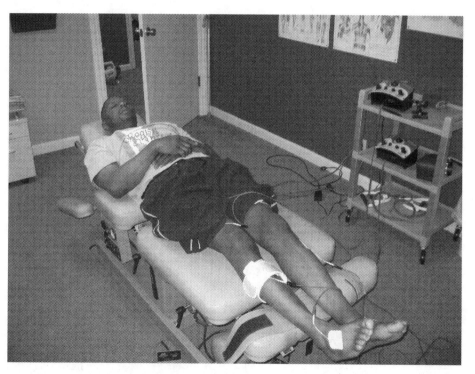

Louis In rehab in San Jose California

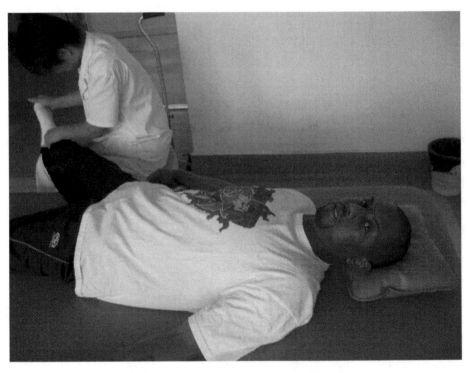

Louis in rehab receiving therapy in China

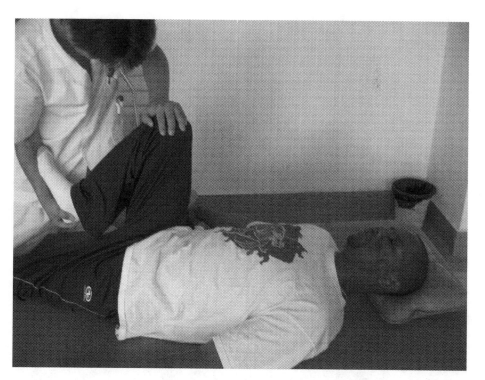

Louis in rehab receiving more therapy in China

Louis sitting up during rehab in San Jose California

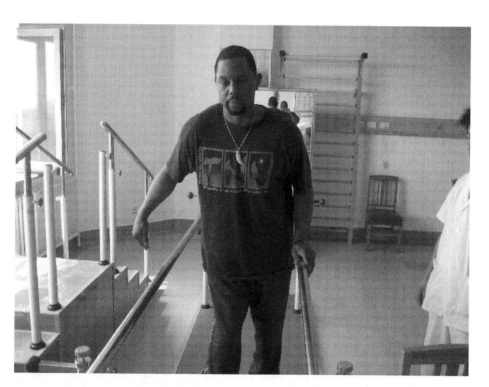

Louis walking therapy in China

Louis doing aquatic therapy facing forward in China

Louis aquatic therapy backward facing

Louis and his sister Tracy in China

Louis and his brother Travis in China

Louis and his wife Shanay in photo shoot

Louis presenting at a speaking engagement in California

Louis speaking in front of a live audience
after making his 10-year comeback

Printed in the United States
by Baker & Taylor Publisher Services